LIVING IN *Luxury*

LIVING IN *Luxury*

INSIDE THE WORLD'S MOST GLAMOROUS HOMES

Alexander V. G. Kraft

FOREWORD BY DONALD J. TRUMP
AFTERWORD BY HENRIETTE VON BOHLEN UND HALBACH

with 150 illustrations, 140 in color

Thames & Hudson

CONTENTS

*To the Kraft clan
(including Professors, Cats and Berties)*

pp. 4–5 (background) The hall of the
Neo-Palladian villa featured on pp. 90–97.

p. 8 An aerial view of the Spanish Colonial
mansion featured on pp. 112–17.

p. 23 The staircase and hall of the
London residence featured on pp. 72–77.

First published in 2008 in hardcover in the United States of America by
Thames & Hudson Inc., 500 Fifth Avenue, New York, New York 10110

thamesandhudsonusa.com

Library of Congress Catalog Card Number 2007910201

ISBN 978-0-500-51417-7

Printed and bound in Singapore by C S Graphics Pte Ltd

FOREWORD

Real estate is far more than dirt, bricks and mortar. Real estate is the source of many fortunes, the core of many businesses. It is a way of life, a passion: if anybody knows that, it's me. *Luxury* properties exert an even stronger fascination. From rappers to royalty, from bellboys to billionaires, everyone likes to dream – and gossip – about mind-boggling super-homes and sky-rocketing square-foot prices.

Living in Luxury not only shows some of the world's most spectacular homes (one of them my magnificent Palm Beach estate, currently listed for $125 million), it also offers us a rare insider's look into the fascinating world of luxury real estate, its history, its markets, its mechanisms, and, most important of all, its personalities. Because behind every real-estate success story, a unique personality with a fascinating tale can be found.

Take me, for instance. After learning the essentials of real-estate development from my father, Fred, a builder in Queens and Brooklyn, I became a major player in Manhattan. In the 1980s, everything I touched seemed to turn to gold. I had it all – a yacht, a plane, a best-selling book. Then the real-estate market crashed – and I owed billions of dollars. In the midst of the crash, I passed a beggar on the street and realized he was worth billions more than me. And nowadays? I am on top again, with landmark properties in New York, Palm Beach and the rest of the world, hotels, casinos, 'the best club anywhere in the world', a record-breaking TV show, best-selling books, and, and, and….

You will find many more fascinating tales in this book. From Prince Alfonso zu Hohenlohe, the founding father of Marbella who discovered the Spanish resort when his father's Rolls Royce broke down, to the English Grosvenor family who acquired immense wealth and noble titles through the ownership of large chunks of London for centuries. Delve in – and be amazed!

DONALD J. TRUMP

PREFACE

Welcome to the wonderful world of luxury property

An apartment in Paris or New York for the shopping sprees, a villa in the South of France or on the Costa Smeralda for soaking up the sun when it's raining in the city, or a romantic castle in Burgundy or Shropshire for those cosy winter evenings.… Who does not dream of having a different base for every season; a property to suit every mood, or momentary need? Even those who already own more houses than other people own cars can't seem to get enough. There always seems to be a hot new location where everybody who's anybody suddenly congregates, and where real-estate prices are sky-rocketing. When to actually live in all those properties? Well, that's a different story.…

Luxury real estate exerts a powerful attraction on all kinds of people, whether they can only fantasize or whether they are already investors. Kings have ruined themselves and their countries to build fairytale castles; Greek refugees have become among the most wealthy and prolific property purchasers in the world; pop stars now show off their mansions on MTV's *Cribs*. Meanwhile the recent sale of a London penthouse for a reported £115 million – the annual budget of a small country – made the headlines in tabloids and financial press alike.

Why are luxury properties so fascinating? First of all there is, let's face it, a good deal of voyeurism involved. A luxury property is usually, in one form or another, an expression of the personality and taste of its owner. Whether it belongs to a self-made businessman wanting to flaunt his newly acquired financial and social status or a noble dynasty struggling to adapt to the realities of the twenty-first century, a luxury property will often tell you a good deal about its proprietor, as we shall see when looking at the example of J. Paul Getty, in his time the richest man in the world.

Naturally, there is also a great deal of money involved. By its very nature, a luxury property is a significant financial asset. Some owners, such as the legendary Rothschild family, were able not only to preserve their wealth, but actually to increase it, through the acquisition of luxury properties. And, of course, successful real-estate transactions have also been the very foundation of fortunes in the first place; if you don't believe me, just ask Donald J. Trump. For other owners, however, the financial burden of maintaining a prestige property has led to desperate measures, including the dismantling and burying of vintage cars in the middle of the night, in the case of Lord Brocket and his family seat, Brocket Hall.

Myths abound in the fabulous world of prime real estate. We shall see how one project took almost thirty years and the changing ownership of a Hollywood legend, several financial investors and a Fortune 500 billionaire to come finally to fruition. But what are the mechanisms behind the myths? How do international hotspots develop? Where does it make sense to invest long-term? These are some of the questions we shall be considering.

In addition to helping the reader understand the background to and inner workings of the luxury real-estate market, the book aims to give some practical guidance for navigating this highly complicated terrain. Sometimes even those who are involved in the business – be it as owner, investor or advisor – do not seem to appreciate the many nuances. Of course, the book is intended to be neither a scholarly volume nor a 'how to become a property expert in five easy lessons' guide. What we shall do is look at luxury real estate's most important aspects, explore some of its major mechanisms, and, of course, peek at some sumptuous properties along the way. Enjoy!

ALEXANDER V. G. KRAFT

INTRODUCTION

THE MANY DIFFERENT ASPECTS OF LUXURY REAL ESTATE: OF PRINCES, BILLIONAIRES AND PAY PHONES

Medieval German castles, French châteaux, Swiss chalets, grand London townhouses, Malibu beachfront homes: the list of types of luxury real estate could go on and on. But prime real estate not only comes in many different forms, it also caters to many different needs and aspirations. Let's be honest, nobody actually needs a home with 1,000 square metres of living space (unless you plan to house your entire extended family under one roof) and, with the possible exception of movie producers, very few people actually need a thirty-seat home-cinema. Far from being a simple dwelling, then, a luxury property is also a status symbol, an expression of personality and individual taste, and, of course, a considerable financial investment. Such properties – long the source of political, social and financial power – have also often played a decisive role in the fate of their owners. Many famous names and stories are intrinsically linked with properties and real-estate markets. Indeed, single personalities have been responsible for making a city, a region or even an entire country an international hotspot.

How great personalities have shaped entire regions: the legend of Marbella and Prince Alfonso zu Hohenlohe-Langenburg Until the 1940s Marbella was nothing but a little village of some 900 inhabitants on the Spanish Costa del Sol. According to legend, it owes its fame in large part to fate, which decided that one day the Rolls Royce of a visiting German prince would break down there during a motoring trip the prince and his son and heir Alfonso were taking.

Alfonso Hohenlohe – or to be a little more precise, His Serene Highness Alfonso Maximiliano Victorio Eugenio Alexandro Maria Pablo de la Santísima Trinidad y todos los Santos zu Hohenlohe-Langenburg, son of Prince Max Egon zu Hohenlohe-Langenburg and Maria de la Piedad de Yturbe y Scholtz, Marquesa de Belvis de las Navas – fell in love with the place and decided to stay. In 1946 he acquired substantial amounts of land and established his own private residence at Finca Santa Margarita. The prince's new home soon became a magnet for his many friends from other distinguished European families, who visited him in ever-increasing numbers. In 1954 he opened the now-legendary Marbella Club Hotel, thus fulfilling his dream of transforming his property into an exclusive club-resort.

Located on Marbella beach, with charming traditional Spanish houses set in hectares of sprawling grounds containing some 23,000 trees, the Marbella Club didn't feel like a conventional hotel; it still felt like a private retreat. Prince Hohenlohe was able to convince his noble friends and a steadily increasing number of international jetsetters to visit the resort and enjoy a luxurious lifestyle in a carefree setting. Soon, more and more of these illustrious visitors also began to acquire real estate in and around the Club, thereby laying the foundation for the town's incredible growth.

Alfonso de Mora y Aragón, brother of Queen Fabiola of Belgium, was a frequent visitor. So was Saudi Arabian Prince, later King, Fahd, who arrived on the scene in 1974, purportedly after having broken the bank of the casino at Monte Carlo (of course, he did not arrive alone; the entourage that set up residence with him is reported to have consisted of as many as a thousand people at a time). Other notable residents have included Count Rudolf von Schönburg-Glauchau, who managed the Marbella Club for Prince Hohenlohe; Countess Gunilla von Bismarck; international businessman and millionaire Adnan Khashoggi; and Hollywood legend Sean Connery.

Where the rich and famous congregate, others tend to follow, and Marbella was no exception. The former village developed

Marbella Club, Marbella, Spain

into an international resort, and has since then remained one of the most important luxury real-estate markets in Europe.

However, what may sound like a simple and straightforward recipe – take one high-society jetsetter, let him invest part of his fortune in a luxurious real-estate venture in a charming yet undiscovered location, make his equally rich and famous friends follow him, and, voilà, you have a new international hotspot – is by no means a guarantee for success. Having a great name, or an even greater fortune, does not necessarily mean anything in the highly specialized universe of prime real estate, which functions according to its very own laws. Many luxury real-estate ventures – or should one say adventures – have had a chequered history, with frustrated dreams, ruined investors and frequent changes of ownership before finally taking off.

The mysterious mechanisms of the luxury real-estate market: the case of Domaine de Terre Blanche
One project with a colourful history is the Domaine de Terre Blanche, today one of the world's premier golf developments. Situated in the Provence region of southern France, it is approximately 45 minutes from the international airport in Nice, 30 minutes from Cannes and its famous Croisette, and one hour from the beaches of St Tropez. Today the development comes complete with a Four Seasons resort, two championship golf courses designed by Dave Thomas, a 3,000-square-metre (32,000 sq. ft) spa and a highly exclusive private villa community.

The development was originally the vision of actor Sean Connery, who had picked up a passion for golf during the filming of *Goldfinger*. In 1979 he bought the 265-hectare (650-acre) property of Domaine de Terre Blanche with the intention of setting up a golf resort. For a number of reasons, including infamous French bureaucracy, these plans were never realized and the property was sold on to a Swedish financial group in 1993. Despite several attempts, these investors fared no better than Connery, and by the late 1990s the project had still not materialized.

The property was then acquired by entrepreneur Dietmar Hopp, probably best known for co-founding the German software giant SAP. Hopp was a passionate golfer, with a 9 handicap, and had already founded one of Germany's most distinguished golf clubs, St Leon Rot, host of the 'Deutsche Bank – SAP Open' (which seems to be won every year by Tiger Woods!). Hopp also owned a villa in a golf development in southern Spain, but had grown disenchanted with it when it became overrun by golfers from the development's hotel. At Terre Blanche he saw the opportunity to build the golf resort of his dreams.

Being a Fortune 500 billionaire and having business interests in many different companies and fields ranging from soccer clubs to breweries, Hopp brought not only considerable financial resources but also a good deal of entrepreneurial experience to the table. A decade and an investment of more than €122 million later, Domaine de Terre Blanche has set new standards

Domaine de Terre Blanche, Provence, France

for golf developments in Europe and has finally – some thirty years after its conception – become one of Europe's most distinguished high-end real-estate developments.

Luxury real estate as the expression of an owner's personality: J. Paul Getty and Sutton Place
A luxury property is usually, of course, much more than a financial venture, or the realization of somebody's vision: it is almost always an expression, too, of its owner's personality. Whether the Scandinavian wife of a self-made billionaire making her earliest childhood dreams come true by decorating her newly built Beverly Hills mansion along the lines of Sun King Louis XIV, or the son of a legendary German jetsetter preferring to relax on a self-designed piece of felt, a luxury home also tells the story of its proprietor.

The English country house Sutton Place was for many years the home of Jean Paul Getty. After joining his father's Oklahoma oil business in 1914, Getty had founded his own business, the Getty Oil Company (Tulsa). The success of this venture made it possible for him to announce, at the tender age of 24, his intention to retire after making his first million. He in fact went on to turn his company into a global conglomerate, at the same time amassing a stunning collection of art, and eventually becoming known as the richest man in the world.

In 1959 Getty acquired Sutton Place. The house had been built by Sir Richard Weston, one of the most loyal courtiers of King Henry VIII, who granted Weston the ancient manor of Sutton in 1521. The house was in Tudor style, featuring richly decorated façades and large windows. During Getty's ownership, it became the source of much anecdote. Its owner's apparent sense of economy – some have called it stinginess – led to measures that might be considered strange for any home-owner, let alone the world's richest man.

Visitors and staff often commented that interior temperatures at Sutton Place could be far from comfortable: one employee wrote in a letter to her family that temperatures hovered around

Sutton Place, Surrey, England

43°F at Christmas time. Getty also installed a pay-phone booth in the hall, while at the same time placing dial-locks on the other phones around the house. Even in England, where eccentricities tend to be regarded with a benevolent eye, this behaviour was perceived as 'unusual'. (The temperature control was later explained as, rather than being a simple cost-cutting exercise, intended to preserve the antique furniture of Sutton Place. Getty also justified the pay-phone in his autobiography by explaining that visiting workmen, tradesmen, businessmen and so on had been taking advantage of free access to outside lines, including long-distance and overseas operators, and that the Sutton Place phone bills had soared as a result.)

The examples of the Marbella Club, Domaine de Terre Blanche and Sutton Place show just three of the countless and wildly variable facets of prestige real-estate ownership. In the following sections, we shall examine how luxury real estate has evolved over time, what qualifies a home as a luxury property, and how luxury markets function, together with some useful tips on how to navigate those markets.

A BRIEF HISTORY OF LUXURY REAL ESTATE: OF ROMANS, ROTHSCHILDS AND OTHERS

Real estate has long been a source of power as well as an indicator of status. Be it in Ancient Babylon, Egypt, Greece or the Roman Empire, social standing was often a result of, and expressed through, an owner's dwelling.

The prototypes of today's luxury homes: Roman villas as expression of power and status More than 2,000 years before the birth of today's real-estate billionaires, luxury properties were already being used both to create and demonstrate power. The very first luxury homes that bore a resemblance to those of today were probably the villas of the Roman ruling classes. Such patrician properties were found not only in and around Rome but all over the far-reaching empire.

From historic sources, including Pliny the Elder, we learn that there were two different kinds of villa: the 'villa urbana', located in or near a town, and the 'villa rustica', a permanently occupied and self-sufficient farm estate, generating produce such as wine or olive oil, with a villa as centrepiece.

It was not uncommon also for local dignitaries to construct a large building at a strategic point on the road to Rome, allowing them to control the traffic to and from the heart of the empire, and enabling them to hold large-scale functions, thus demonstrating their elevated position to the public. These villas often consisted of several independent structures linked by porticos or enclosed courtyards. In some cases these villas later developed into entire provincial towns.

There seem to have been two general floor plans. The most common blueprint featured separate wings of a building opening onto, and linked by, a portico; sometimes these two wings were extended at right angles so that the portico became an enclosed courtyard. The other type of floor plan, rather than having separate wings, featured a central hall from which aisles extended; such floor plans could often be found in the homes of officials such as magistrates.

Most villas seem to have been timber-framed constructions, though important buildings were usually made from stone. Other building materials included glass and iron: early traces of window glass and iron window grilles have been found.

Villa San Marco in Ancient Stabiae, Italy

'My home is my castle': ownership of land as the basis for aristocracy Following the decline and fall of the Roman Empire, villas ceased to be built and instead fortified structures became a common sight. As times became tougher, defence was a primary consideration. Castles allowed their owners to defend themselves against hostile intrusion and also strategically to control their locality, thus creating a source of power.

The first castles began to appear in the early Middle Ages, around the eleventh century, and at the same time the modern concept of nobility developed in most Western civilizations. This was based on continuous ownership of land – and corresponding titles – through a family clan. The ownership of real estate became an integral part of hereditary privilege, and for centuries property ownership was exclusively limited to the ruling classes, that is to say royalty, nobility and gentry.

As power and wealth were often direct consequences of land possessed, it was natural to wish to increase the former by increasing the latter. Methods were manifold, but conquest, alliances and marriage were common means of expanding both possessions and power.

An example of ownership of land as the basis for aristocracy can be studied in the case of England. Originally, land ownership in England depended, as in other countries and territories, primarily on possession. This, however, abruptly changed with the conquest of England by the Normans in 1066. One of the first acts of William the Conqueror was to decree that he now owned all the land in England by right of conquest. He in turn would grant the right to exploit land to lords of his choosing, such as his Norman officers or those of the English 'natives' who were ready to recognize him as king. This system, known as tenure, would become a key element of the English feudal system. The lords that held their tenure directly from the king (the 'tenants-in-chief' or 'in capite') formed the heart of English aristocracy. They, in turn, would sub-grant the exclusive possession and use of part of the royal tenure to commoners in exchange for goods or services. Such subdivision of the king's land was known as 'subinfeudation', establishing a long chain of tenure, with the king always remaining at the head of the chain. Significant rules of feudal law relating to the rights and obligations of lords and tenants can be found in the 1215 Magna Carta.

Make pow-wow not war: the emergence of the country house As social conditions began to change, it became possible to reduce a property's fortifications and replace them with features that were geared once more towards aesthetic considerations. The Renaissance era saw the re-appearance of luxury homes as we understand them today, that is to say Roman-influenced villas and mansions, complete with ornamental drives, parks and gardens.

Bodiam Castle, East Sussex, England

Agricultural estates became the source of financial and political power. Far from being simple farms, they often included huge portions of land, and also in some cases entire villages and towns. At the heart of such estates large ornamental buildings could be found which served as headquarters. Examples of these types of properties were Villa Farnese and Villa Giulia in Italy, and Hatfield House in England.

Another result of this development was that the ruling classes began to visit, rather than battle, each other (although they did not abandon their fighting habits altogether). In order to be able to stay in touch with other influential persons and families, members of European high society paid visits to each other's country seats. Thus, a social circuit – which could also include interludes in city residences – was born, and still functions to some degree among today's upper classes. These social gatherings allowed visitors to discuss business in an informal atmosphere. Quite often, even affairs of state at the highest level were debated and decided upon with the aid of a good glass of port (or two) and a cigar in the smoking room of a country mansion.

Bigger is better: luxury estate as the ultimate status symbol Of course, luxury homes were not only intended to be meeting places or the logistical headquarters of agricultural estates; they were also intended to reflect the social standing of their owners. As the aristocratic system evolved, so did the buildings, which were now used clearly to communicate their owner's claim to power to the rest of the world. This was a lesson that a certain Nicolas Fouquet had to learn the hard way.

In 1641 Fouquet purchased a small château by the name of Vaux-le-Vicomte, to the southeast of Paris. After becoming finance minister to the young king Louis XIV, Fouquet began to transform Vaux-le-Vicomte into the finest estate in France.

Vaux-le-Vicomte, Seine-et-Marne, France

He enlisted the services of architect Louis Le Vau, painter-decorator Charles Le Brun and landscape gardener André Le Nôtre. The result was spectacular. The finished château and its gardens had no equal in France – the centre of the civilized world at that time – and they were inaugurated on 17 August 1661 with a performance of Molière's play *Les Facheux*, a lavish dinner and an impressive display of fireworks. However, it seems the result was a little too impressive for one of the guests. Unfortunately for Fouquet that guest was the Sun King himself, Louis XIV. After the king was led to believe that the project had been funded with misappropriated public money, Fouquet was arrested, imprisoned for life and his property seized. As Voltaire famously wrote: 'On August 17, at six in the evening, Fouquet was the King of France; at two in the morning, he was nobody.'

Not to be outdone by his (former) finance minister, Louis XIV then began – with the same team of masterminds – to transform a former hunting lodge, built by his father Louis XIII not far from Paris, into the most spectacular palace on earth, the

South parterre, Versailles, France

Château de Versailles. Even by the lavish standards of the Sun King, the construction of the château and its formal gardens – still today probably the most elaborate in the world – was undertaken at an enormous cost. Research estimates that up to 25% of all state funds were used exclusively for Versailles. The total cost today would run into the billions of dollars. This was justified – and still is, by some historians – with the rationale that Versailles was not just a 'leisure property', but the nerve centre of the French court. Undoubtedly one of the main functions of Versailles was to demonstrate in an unparalleled manner – to the French people but also, more importantly, to other sovereigns – Louis XIV's status as a sun-like, absolute king by the grace of God.

Luxury real estate as clever investment: lessons from the Rothschilds

The acquisition of a luxury estate is always, of course, a considerable financial outlay. But even if a residence is acquired primarily as a means of demonstrating status, or for conducting social or financial business, it also constitutes part of the overall investment strategy of its owner. A fascinating example of this aspect of ownership is provided by the family whose name stands like no other for financial genius – the Rothschilds.

The incredible Rothschild saga began with Mayer Amschel Rothschild – a resident of the 'Judengasse', the Jewish ghetto in Frankfurt-am-Main, Germany – who laid the foundation for the family empire with his own successful financial speculations. He soon realized that a family-controlled presence in the world's most important financial centres was indispensable to growing the business successfully. As a consequence, he sent four of his five sons, Salomon Mayer, Nathan Mayer, Calmann Mayer and James Mayer, to Vienna, London, Naples and Paris respectively, to set up branches of the Rothschild firm (the eldest son, Amschel Mayer, was to remain at the home base). Between these five branches, the Rothschilds set up a unique communications network of messengers and carrier pigeons, which established the family's reputation for being a unique source of the most up-to-date news, unequalled even by governments.

The Rothschild fortune was cemented during the Napoleonic wars when the family played a key role in financing the British war effort under the Duke of Wellington. The Rothschilds were able to manifest their unparalleled social ascent by being ennobled in 1816 by Austria's Emperor Francis II. Only two generations later, Nathan's grandson, Natty, received a hereditary peerage from Queen Victoria.

Having acquired their first substantial residences around 1817, the various Rothschild branches began to invest heavily in luxury real estate, both in the city and in the country. James de Rothschild's rue Laffite *hôtel* featured an exquisite wood-panelled salon complete with Renaissance scenes (into which the Rothschild coat of arms was subtly integrated); it also boasted then-state-of-the-art amenities – central heating, running water, gas lighting and central waste tanks. Visibly impressed, the German poet Heinrich Heine described the result as 'the Versailles of the absolute reign of money', while a contemporary Parisian journal, the *Bon Ton*, noted that the property 'seemed to realize the tales of a thousand and one nights. Such luxury is awesome....' This elaborate style would later become known as 'le style Rothschild'. James de Rothschild would also spend substantial sums on his château outside Paris at Ferrières, turning it into a gentleman's retreat complete with stables, a riding track, an orangery and extensive gardens. Other Rothschild châteaux could be found at Boulogne and Suresnes, the latter belonging to James's brother Salomon.

The English Rothschilds were no slouches in the real-estate sector either. When the English prime minister Benjamin Disraeli attended a fête given by Nathan's widow Hannah at their country house Gunnersbury in 1843, it left a strong impression: he later described Gunnersbury as '...a most beautiful park and a villa worthy of an Italian Prince'. However, things did not stop there. Other luxury properties in France, Germany, Italy and Austria were to follow.

Nathaniel de Rothschild, born in London as the fourth child of the founder of the British branch of the family, moved to Paris in 1850 and acquired in 1853 Château Brane Mouton, a vineyard in Pauillac in the Gironde department. He renamed the estate Château Mouton Rothschild – today, needless to say, one of the best-known labels in the world. In 1868 Nathaniel's uncle, James Mayer de Rothschild, acquired the neighbouring – and equally legendary – Château Lafite vineyard.

Other Rothschild residences across Europe included Palace Albert Rothschild in Vienna, a three-storey *hôtel particulier* in French Neo-renaissance style, commissioned by Baron Albert von Rothschild and designed and built by French architect Gabriel-Hippolyte Destailleur. Albert's brother Baron Nathaniel von Rothschild soon followed suit with his Palace Nathaniel Rothschild in Vienna, which French architect Jean Girette designed in French Neo-baroque style. In Italy in 1841, Carl de Rothschild bought the Villa Pignatelli near Naples. In Germany Amschel von Rothschild owned several 'palais' and a castle, the Günthersburg, in the Frankfurt region.

The Rothschilds maintained their astute business sense when indulging in their real-estate shopping sprees. Lionel de Rothschild, for example, is reported to have been singularly unimpressed by some of the vast estates of the nobility when he visited them. He thought Castle Howard, one of England's most famous estates, a 'rather nice place but nothing wonderful. It is in fact just the same as Blenheim, only much smaller.... Altogether not a place worth putting oneself out to go and see.'

When Lionel and his brothers were buying land in the 1840s, they did so, at least in part, with an eye to simple investment. Lionel made the following calculations with regard to a property

he sought to acquire in Creslow, Buckinghamshire, in 1844: 'I should not mind having it, as a 33 per cent purchase would pay me 3 per cent, and there are so many little places round it which might be thought worth the money, that the whole together might be made to pay a fair rate of interest.' Considerations of a similar nature applied when the Rothschilds exploited tempting opportunities to acquire property following the bankruptcy of the Duke of Buckingham in 1848 and the death of Sir John Dashwood the following year. It is estimated that the Rothschild family eventually invested up to one third of their entire wealth in real estate, while the other two thirds were equally divided into art and financial assets.

The end of an era – and the beginning of modern times
Between the sixteenth and early nineteenth centuries, the country-house culture flourished all over Europe. However, in the twentieth century the history of 'luxury homes' took a dramatic turn.

The decline of the country house began in the nineteenth century, which saw immense social and political changes across Europe. As a result of industrialization, many country dwellers left their homes to find better-paid jobs in the cities. At the same time, the agricultural depression, notably in England in the 1870s, made it increasingly difficult to run large country estates along the old lines.

This development was significantly accelerated by World War I, when many members of country-house staff had to join the war effort either as combatants or as workers in ammunition factories and such like. Sadly, many of these never returned, which in turn made it increasingly difficult to keep large estates running. The final blow for the country-house culture came with World War II, which saw unparalleled destruction and loss of human life all over Europe.

Those of the large estates that were not damaged or destroyed in the war were often requisitioned by government for official use as military installations, hospitals, shelters, and so on. If and when they were returned to their owners after the war, they were usually in very poor condition, requiring huge investments to return them to an inhabitable state. In some parts of Europe, of course, many estates were completely destroyed, or subsequently became casualties of the postwar political restructuring of Europe: a lot of estate owners in Central and Eastern Europe were forced to flee and leave their ancestral homes behind.

In Western Europe, many owners who were still in possession of their old homes found that they had lost both their heirs and their staff in the war; agricultural income from the estates had dramatically dropped and could not support the upkeep, let alone the renovation, of the large ornamental mansions at the heart of the estates; and extremely heavy taxes and death duties introduced at that time gave the final deathblow. Thus, many houses were sold and converted into schools, hospitals and other institutions. Some houses, like Cliveden and Hartwell House in England, were turned into hotels. Others were completely demolished, and their contents and building materials – such as wood panelling, fireplaces and stones – sold off. According to *The Latest Country Houses* by John Martin Robinson, between 1875 and 1975 1,116 country houses in the United Kingdom were destroyed, some quarter of the total. The worst periods were after World War I and World War II. The peak was in 1955, when 76 houses were destroyed.

WHAT IS A LUXURY HOME TODAY?

When does a house become a 'luxury home'? This may sound like an easy one: 'Well, of course, a big villa in the sun, with marble floors, swimming pool, the works….' But while size, location and materials are undoubtedly important factors in distinguishing 'luxury' homes from their 'average' cousins, they are by no means the only factors that need to be taken into consideration.

Some factors may seem to be objective and some subjective, but when one looks a little closer the two are rather harder to distinguish. For example, size and location might seem to be objective factors, but in fact they are not so easily determinable. 'The bigger the better' is not necessarily a universal truth in the world of luxury real estate. As we shall see, many estates can actually prove to be too large from a maintenance perspective, and can become the source of financial ruin rather than being a profitable asset. A charming pied-à-terre with only 100 square metres of living space in a city like Paris can turn out be a much better, and more enjoyable, investment, than a damp castle with 1,000 square metres of living space and grounds of 500 hectares, in, let's say, the Scottish highlands. So when does 'a lot' become 'too much'? This is a question we will examine at length (see p. 21).

A 'good location' can also be a tricky factor to determine. Plentiful are the stories of supposedly 'hot' real-estate markets that have seen a brief period of frenzied investment, only to be followed by a crash in price from which they've never recovered. So what are the telltale signs that allow us to determine whether a market has good long-term prospects? This, too, is a point we shall later consider (see p. 164).

One factor that is most often cited as the most important in ascertaining whether a piece of real estate qualifies as a luxury property is its image, its standing. But how can something as subjective as the 'image' of a property be determined? The perception of luxury, especially in the real-estate world, still varies widely depending on influences such as education, social background and, of course, national culture.

It is most interesting – and entertaining – to see how different cultures place different importance on the various factors that are used to qualify a property as a 'luxury home'. Although there is, of course, no such thing as 'the typical American buyer' or 'the typical German buyer', it is still possible to observe certain patterns in the behaviour of home-buyers from different cultures. These disparities become most evident in the way prospective buyers examine a property they are considering acquiring. That these differences are not the product of the vivid imagination of the author, but are, on the contrary, quite real, can be seen in the parallel universe of luxury hotels, which cater in a similar way to the varying notions of luxury of a clientele from diverse countries and cultures.

Luxury is comfort: the American way of life In America, of course, everything is generally a little bit bigger – the main courses, the limousines, the breast implants…. And America is also the home of the 'drive-thru'; the place where anything from pizzas to escorts can be ordered via phone or internet and be delivered conveniently to one's doorstep.

American buyers of luxury homes will usually check first to see whether a property offers all the comforts and amenities that are indispensable to their lifestyle. Whereas in many European countries a luxury home such as a French bastide or Tuscan rustico could easily contain seven or eight bedrooms with only two bathrooms, such a thing would be unthinkable in the US. Nowadays no home in the States would be considered a luxury home without en-suite bathrooms and dressing rooms for every bedroom. Other features that most Americans would naturally expect include air-conditioning, home-cinemas, large garages and even larger pools.

This understanding of luxury is also reflected in the way most American luxury hotels operate. While many of these still tend to have a rather uniform look, they all offer a very high standard of amenity, including not only air-conditioning and cable TV, which nowadays can be found in even the cheapest motels, but also plasma TVs, wireless internet access, 24-hour room service, in-room massages, separate dressing areas, luxury bathrooms with separate toilets, showers and bathtubs, and so on – all amenities geared towards making life as comfortable as possible.

'A rather charming pile': luxury according to the British In England, on the other hand, 'understatement' has long been the watchword. Things need to have a little patina to appeal to the truly British mind. (There are famous stories of the English aristocrat who hands over his new pair of custom-made shoes to the butler, who is to wear them until they have acquired a sufficiently 'worn' look; equally, it was not uncommon for a handful of stones to be placed in the pockets of a new suit after its delivery from the family tailor on Savile Row, so that it would look like a long-serving part of a gentleman's wardrobe rather than a brand-new acquisition.) In contrast to the prospective American purchaser, who might first examine the bedrooms and

bathrooms, an English visitor will usually look first for the property's noteworthy architectural and historical features. Their main consideration is not so much comfort as charm. A cosy sitting room with a historic fireplace will often help the English buyer forget the fact that the bathrooms are rather small, the attic damp and the garage non-existent.

This attitude is also reflected in the luxury hotel industry in the UK. Traditional 'grand hotels' of the old school still dominate. Though they are increasingly adopting the slick service model of their American counterparts, they continue to specialize in tasteful antique furnishings, historic surroundings and personal – rather than standardized – service.

'Quality made in Germany': luxury according to the Germans (and Swiss)

Porsche, Mercedes, BMW and Audi are counted among the world's best cars, but a Ferrari is considered more sporty, a Rolls Royce more luxurious, a Jaguar more elegant. Clothing brands such as BOSS, Escada and Joop are equally regarded as high-quality staples for any wardrobe, but they are not *haute couture* or cutting edge. 'Quality made in Germany' may not have the biggest sex appeal, but it certainly stands for reliability and value for money.

While the English may be on the hunt for the most romantic features of a property, and Americans may check out a property's amenities, a German might pay his first visit to … the basement. He will carefully examine the date and make of the central heating system, ask the seller or agent detailed questions about the state of the plumbing, and take a close look at the quality of the kitchen. If the buyer detects the presence of world-renowned German brands such as Poggenpohl for kitchens, Hansgrohe for taps or Vaillant for heating systems, he will be reassured that the property really does offer the highest possible degree of quality and, thus, luxury.

This view is also reflected in the German luxury hotel scene, which is not known for the most state-of-the-art amenities or the most impressive historic grandeur, but has always had a very solid, service-minded approach, offering its guests good value. Not surprisingly, many of the world's best hotels, clubs and restaurants are run by German managers.

'Dreams of a thousand and one nights': luxury according to the Middle Eastern buyer

Middle Eastern buyers tend to have the most traditional approach to luxury: precious materials equal luxury. These buyers will look for marble floors (the rarer the marble the better), gold taps, sumptuous wallpaper and intricate window dressings. For them 'more is more': the most exquisite finishes, the biggest floor plans, the most incredible projects.

Nowhere can this phenomenon be better observed than in the United Arab Emirates, which is currently witnessing a true 'real-estate gold rush' as the government invests heavily in superlative developments to position the country as a business, tourist and luxury real-estate destination, thus lessening its dependence on oil revenues which are predicted to run out over the next twenty-five years. These developments include, to name but a few, the world's tallest skyscraper, the Burj Dubai, as well as the world's largest manmade islands, The World and The Palms. The World – a collection of islands shaped like the continents – is located off the coast of Dubai. The 300 individual islands in the complex are divided into four categories – private homes, estate homes, dream resorts and community islands. The only means of transportation between them is boat or helicopter. Pricing is expected to begin at US$6.85 million. The Palm Islands are also off the Dubai coast, and are designed in the shape of date-palm trees, consisting of a trunk and a crown with seventeen fronds. Apart from some sixty luxury hotels, they will contain approximately four thousand exclusive residential villas, one thousand unique water homes and five thousand shoreline apartments. Sales will be made on a freehold basis, which entitles nationals and expats the right to sell, lease or rent their property at their own discretion. An additional incentive is that the property – other than offering guaranteed year-round sunshine – is tax-free and enables owners to become Dubai residents with corresponding tax-free status.

In the Middle East, too, the concept of 'best of the best' visible luxury is echoed in the local hotel scene. As John Kampfner wrote in *The Guardian* (12 March 2005): 'I have just arrived at the Emirates Palace Hotel [in Abu Dhabi], much more palace than hotel, and one of the most jaw-dropping places to stay on the planet. This is a monument to excess and opulence in a region where if you've got billions you flaunt them.… To appreciate the monolithic structure, you have to take in the stats. Here are just a few: this marble and granite palace stretches more than a kilometre from end to end. It contains 6,000 square metres of gold leaf, has 7,000 doors, 12,000 signs and 1,002 chandeliers made with Swarovski crystals. The centre of the palace is dominated by a grand atrium, the biggest in the world. Its gold gilded dome, one of 114 in the building, outstrips the one in St Paul's Cathedral.'

'The Gucci crowd': luxury according to the in-crowd

To a growing number of clients, luxury is not necessarily judged by considerations of comfort, charm, quality or preciousness, as defined above, but rather by the lifestyle on offer. This is expressed through a unique design theme, which instantly creates a vibe of its own. The names of the architects and developers involved have become 'brands', trusted institutions promising full-service 'lifestyle management', trendiness and a high level of sophistication.

This new trend has its origins in the hotel business, where in the 1990s visionaries such as Andrée Putman, Ian Schrager and Jacques Garcia started to create highly individual, fully designed spaces catering to the taste of a young, professional, international crowd with an appetite for something fresh. Hotels such as the Costes in Paris, One Aldwych in London and the Hudson in New York quickly generated a loyal following, which prompted a worldwide boom in design hotels.

The trend has now caught on in the luxury real-estate business. Developers are teaming up with star designers and architects such as Philippe Starck, Herzog & de Meuron and Rem Koolhaas to create signature complexes that offer a fully designed lifestyle. As almost always in the real-estate business, this movement has emerged from the creative centre of the new world – New York. At the time of writing, more than a dozen architecturally significant projects are underway there that are seen as worthy heirs to the icons of the mid-twentieth-century 'International Style'.

From Harry's Bar to New York apartments: Cipriani Club Residences

In international society, the name Cipriani has an almost mystical ring. In 1918, a young Giuseppe Cipriani answered an ad for a position at the Hotel des Alpes in Madonna di Campiglio, Italy. Signore Cipriani did not know anything about restaurants, but he acquired a comprehensive knowledge the hard way, by working in a number of different hotels over the next twelve years. On 13 May 1931 he and a rich Bostonian by the name of Harry Pickering embarked on a business venture that would soon become a legend – Harry's Bar in Venice, Italy.

The story goes that Pickering had been a loyal customer at the Hotel Europa, where Cipriani was working as a bartender, but suddenly stopped turning up. When Cipriani ran into the young man one day and asked him why he was no longer frequenting the bar, Pickering confessed that he was broke as his family had cut off his allowance due to his fondness for trouble in general, and drinks in particular. To help him out, Cipriani loaned him a sizeable chunk of cash – about 10,000 lire (some US$5,000 at that time). Two years later, Pickering walked back into the Hotel Europa, ordered a drink at the bar and handed over 10,000 lire with the words: 'Mr Cipriani, thank you. Here's the money. And to show you my appreciation, here's 40,000 more – enough to open a bar. We'll call it Harry's Bar.'

Located on Calle Vallaresso, just a few steps from the Piazza San Marco, the tiny 30-square-metre (320 sq. ft) bar – and later restaurant, combining exquisite service with no-nonsense Italian cuisine – soon developed a cult following, and became the hangout of choice for international aristocrats, film stars, artists and writers. One famous regular from 1949 onwards was Ernest Hemingway, who immortalized the bar in *Across the River and Into the Trees*. Another notable patron was the Aga Khan, who had to be carried to the door in his own armchair and always ate the same thing, caviar followed by ravioli. Film legend Orson Welles would down two bottles of Dom Perignon at one sitting, while author and society darling Truman Capote liked to order the now-famous prawn sandwiches.

Two culinary staples originated at Harry's Bar: the Bellini and the Beef Carpaccio. The Bellini, a mixture of white peach juice and sparkling Prosecco, is named after the fifteenth-century Venetian painter Giovanni Bellini. The Carpaccio is a dish of 'trimmed sirloin sliced wafer thin and dressed with a Jackson Pollock spray of mayonnaise mixed with lemon juice'. It was invented for an Italian contessa who was on a diet free of cooked meat, and it too was named after an Italian painter – Vittore Carpaccio, famous for his love of deep reds.

Giuseppe eventually fulfilled his dream of having his own hotel when he opened the Hotel Cipriani in Venice in 1958, leaving Harry's Bar to his son Arrigo. The fame and glamour of Harry's Bar were soon transplanted to other parts of the world: Arrigo and son Giuseppe opened the Cipriani restaurant in New York, followed by Harry Cipriani on Fifth Avenue, Downtown Cipriani in SoHo, Cipriani 42nd Street, and Rainbow by Cipriani in Rockefeller Plaza. Other outposts can be found in London and Hong Kong.

Now, some 75 years after the founding of Harry's Bar, the Cipriani clan is venturing into luxury real estate. An impressive, Neo-classical building on Wall Street, which once housed the National City Bank and later the Regent Hotel, has been converted into the first 'Cipriani Club Residence'. A classic Beaux-Arts masterpiece, 55 Wall Street was originally designed by Isaiah Rogers and later expanded by McKim, Mead & White, architects of such New York landmarks as the Pierpont Morgan Library and The Harvard Club. Masterminded by Giuseppe Cipriani, the current head of the family dynasty, the apartment building is designed by architects Tsao & McKown. The new owners can choose from three different residential styles – Classic, Sleek or Eclectic. In addition to luxury staples such as doorman service and an on-site fitness club, residents can make use of butler and housekeeping service, personal shopping and delivery services, and, on demand, even more personalized services such as dog sitting, mail handling and grocery shopping.

From Studio 54 to cheap boutique hotels to lifestyle living: Ian Schrager

For some forty years, Ian Schrager has been one of the most interesting personalities on the hospitality scene. He first became known as the co-owner of Studio 54, New York's legendary discothèque of the late 1970s and early '80s. Located at 254 West 54th Street, Studio 54 was opened on April 1976 by Schrager and his college friend Steve Rubell. The club's promoter Carmen d'Alessio was able to align an impressive array of celebrities for the opening night: Margaux Hemingway, Donald Trump, Bianca Jagger and Brooke Shields partied away, while other stars such as Mick Jagger and Frank Sinatra did not make it inside, thus setting the precedent for Studio 54's idiosyncratic door policy.

In time, the club became famous not only for the hedonistic lifestyle it promoted but also for drug consumption and dubious financial practices. Following a raid by Federal agents and arrest

Ian Schrager's 40 Bond, New York

for drug possession, Schrager and Rubell were sentenced to prison. That, however, did not deter them for long, and they soon turned their attention to the hotel business. With the opening of Morgan's Hotel in 1984, they would introduce a new concept later to become known as 'the boutique hotel'.

With their newly founded Morgans Hotel Group, they opened other successful hotels, the Royalton and Paramount, which became renowned for their 'lobby socializing'. Apart from their glamorous lobbies functioning as watering holes, these hotels offered 'cheap chic' – affordable luxury presented in a stylish and sophisticated environment. Schrager's 'urban resorts', the Mondrian and Delano in Miami, became jetset staples just like his other ventures, including the Sanderson and the St Martins Lane Hotel in London.

Schrager is now venturing into luxury residential real estate with two high-end projects in New York. His first, 50 Gramercy Park North, designed by London architect John Pawson, consists of luxury residences adjacent to the city's only private park. It promises its owners complete lifestyle management, including a fully staffed household 24 hours a day, seven days a week. Schrager is also in the process of developing 40 Bond, designed by Herzog & de Meuron, and combining luxury apartments and townhouses – the first townhouses to be built in New York City in decades. In addition, Schrager is planning residential and hotel projects in New York and Miami, as well as an entire residential community with recreational and entertainment facilities in Las Vegas.

From cool hotels to cooler apartments: André Balazs

Another hip hotelier who has changed the hotel landscape and is now branching out into residential real estate is André Balazs. The son of Hungarian immigrants, Balazs studied at Cornell and Columbia before going on to found a biotech company with his doctor/professor father. The proceeds from this were used to invest in New York nightclubs, but Balazs really became a name when he began investing in hotels. The first was the famous – or infamous – Château Marmont in Beverly Hills.

Modelled after a château from the French Loire Valley, Château Marmont was opened in 1929 as a grand apartment block and was advertised as the first earthquake-proof building in Los Angeles. Only two years later it was converted into a hotel, and soon became a magnet for Hollywood stars, high society and celebrities from all walks of life. Errol Flynn entertained some very young female company there, Greta Garbo hid herself away, Marilyn Monroe and Marlon Brando stayed there (though not together); Helmut Newton lived, photographed and eventually died there, as did famously John Belushi after a drug overdose. Balazs acquired the hotel, which had become a little tired, and carefully updated and refreshed it, without, however, introducing any radical changes that might turn off its loyal clientele who adored the hotel's quirkiness.

Another famous Balazs property is The Mercer, which opened its doors in New York's SoHo in 1997 and has since become a hangout for Hollywood actors, rock stars, models and the young in-crowd. Offering casual elegance in a relaxed downtown atmosphere, it immediately stood in sharp contrast to the city's established 'grand hotels'. Distinctive amenities included a CD and DVD lending library, minibar snacks from New York's famous deli Dean & Deluca, and a restaurant, the Mercer Kitchen, run by celebrity chef Jean-Georges Vongerichten and serving French-New American cuisine. Other Balazs properties include Sunset Beach on Shelter Island and The Standard in Los Angeles.

With new projects 40 Mercer and M40, Balazs has now turned his attention to luxury residential real estate. Designed by revered French architect Jean Nouvel, whose previous buildings include the Cartier Foundation for Contemporary Art in Paris, 40 Mercer is a modern glass and steel structure located in SoHo. The *New York Times* called the 2001 approval of the structure by the city's Landmarks Preservation Commission one of 'breathtaking importance for the future of architecture in New York'. The 40-unit ultra-luxury condominiums are located on a former parking lot on Grand Street between Broadway and Mercer Street, and are priced from $2.5 million to $13.5 million. The apartments feature unusual luxury amenities, including moveable walls: since terraces or roof gardens are impossible in this location, Balazs has created enormous, motor-driven, sliding glass walls that allow owners to open up their unit and thus 'bring a terrace indoors'. A bathhouse has also been specially designed for the amenity floor, which in addition includes a T-shaped, 15-metre (50 ft) lap pool, a wood-panelled gymnasium, and a lounge with catering bar and projection screens, available for private functions. Two penthouses feature 20-square-metre (210 sq. ft) terraces with outdoor swimming pools.

Other developments in New York
At 80 South Street, Santiago Calatrava has created one of the most fascinating structures ever to be built. Ten glass cubes, each housing a four-storey townhouse, are stacked one on top of the other between two 255-metre-tall (835 ft) poles. Each townhouse contains over 930 square metres (10,000 sq. ft) of interior space, as well as over 150 square metres (1,600 sq. ft) of private garden. Top-of-the-line finishes and fixtures, high-level security, a full round-the-clock staff, and nearby heliports and marinas enhance what has already been declared 'an individual work of genius' (*New York Times*). Prices start at $29 million, considered by some to be a snip for the opportunity to own a piece of rarely available Manhattan waterfront real estate as well as a piece of monumental sculpture that will surely take its place in architectural history.

Another significant recent residential project is the Urban Glass House, one of architect Philip Johnson's last designs. Right on time for his 100th birthday, architect Annabelle Selldorf finished the project, and it opened in July 2006 in lower Manhattan.

Santiago Calatrava's 80 South Street, New York

The global spread of the luxury trend
The current wave of design projects is now spreading from New York to the rest of the world. Santiago Calatrava's Turning Torso, a 190-metre-high (625 ft) sculptural skyscraper in the provincial Swedish town of Malmö, features – in addition to offices and conference facilities – exclusive apartments designed by Samark Arkitektur.

In London, the Yoo group consists of an illustrious coterie including the internationally renowned designer Philippe Starck, the high-end real-estate developer John Hitchcox and Jade Jagger, the jeweller and jetsetting daughter of Mick Jagger. Yoo creates fully designed luxury apartments with options such as Minimal, Culture, Nature and Classic, in hot locations around the world including London, Miami, Sydney, Buenos Aires, Hamburg, New York and Madrid.

From fashion to real estate
Another emerging trend now sees fashion designers beginning to dabble in real estate. At 20 Pine Street in New York, full-service luxury condominiums are being offered, with interiors designed by Armani Casa. The maestro himself is scheduled to open his first Armani hotel in the world's tallest building, the Burj Dubai. This building will cost its owner, Emaar Properties, approximately US$1 billion to construct, and the Armani Hotel will be located in the lower 37 storeys. It will feature, in addition to 172 hotel rooms, 492 residences for permanent guests.

Other fashion houses have already started to create signature hotels, including the Bulgari group (with a stunning hotel in Milan), the Ferragamo group and Versace. While these are for the time being concentrating on hotels, it may only be a matter of time before they turn their attention to residential projects as well.

From major hotel groups to real estate
One of the most revered hotel groups among the international cognoscenti is the Amanresorts group. Amanresorts was one of the first to home in on a lifestyle experience, focussing on shared values such as a passion for faraway places, interest in different cultures and, of course, appetite for elegant luxury. Each of the Amanresorts – in far-flung locations such as Thailand, Bali, Morocco and the Caribbean – is quite different in look, mood and guest experience. At the same time, the company has managed to achieve what was deemed impossible before: building both aesthetically pleasing and environmentally friendly resorts. The service is also first-class and includes such amenities as a personal massage therapist on standby 24 hours a day, and a private butler. Founder Adrian Zecha has created a cult following of loyal customers who travel from resort to resort, the so-called 'Aman junkies'.

For those who want to take the Aman-lifestyle a step further and make it a permanent feature, the group has created Amanvillas, luxury residences adjacent to Amanresorts that benefit from both the Aman-location and all its services. Amanvillas can be acquired at Amanyara (Turks and Caicos Islands), Amanpulo (Pamalican Island, Philippines), Amangani (Jackson Hole, Wyoming, USA) and Amanjena (Marrakech, Morocco).

Other companies that are following this business model – i.e. creating real-estate opportunities at premier resort destinations that benefit from hotel amenities – are established luxury hotel groups such as the Ritz-Carlton and the Four Seasons. In addition to offering traditional real-estate ownership for villas within their resorts, some of these groups also offer alternative options such as 'fractional ownership' or 'destination clubs' (see p. 171).

THE RIGHT SIZE: WHEN DOES 'A LOT' BECOME 'TOO MUCH'?

As German count Christoph Douglas once put it: 'Have you ever tried to maintain four hectares of roof?' While the idea of luxury real estate is extremely alluring, the reality can be quite a different story. The case of Brocket Hall in Hertfordshire, England (see also p. 98), clearly demonstrates where the pressures of owning high-maintenance property can lead.

The cautionary tale of Brocket Hall This impressive mansion has been through many incarnations, its earliest roots dating back as far as 1239. Its current form was designed by renowned architect James Paine for Sir Mathew Lamb in 1760. The son of Sir Mathew became the first Lord Melbourne, largely through the dedicated 'efforts' of his wife, who happened to be a mistress of a frequent visitor to Brocket Hall, the Prince Regent, later King George IV. Romantic liaisons seemed to flourish at Brocket Hall. The wife of the second Lord Melbourne had a great passion for the poet Lord Byron and is said to have fallen from her horse at the shock of seeing his funeral cortege passing the Brocket estate (by all accounts, she had not known of his death until that moment). Her husband became the first Prime Minister to Queen Victoria, with whom he struck up a close friendship and who often stayed at the Hall. On Melbourne's death in 1848, the Hall passed to his sister, who later married Lord Palmerston. Palmerston, in turn, eventually became Prime Minister. He died in somewhat bizarre circumstances, allegedly involving a chambermaid – if true, an incident typical of Brocket Hall's colourful history.

In more recent times, the Hall passed into the possession of Charlie Brocket, also known as Sir Charles Ronald George Nall-Cain, 3rd Baron Brocket. His father had died when he was just nine years old, and the title of Lord Brocket passed to him at the age of 21 on his grandfather's death. At that time, he also inherited the slowly deteriorating ruin that Brocket Hall had become

after World War II. As his grandfather had left him nothing much else apart from the crumbling pile, Brocket had to explore other avenues to save his ancestral home.

Instead of selling or demolishing the Hall, Lord Brocket borrowed US$10 million from the American Express Company to convert the 46-bedroom manor on 405 hectares (1,000 acres) into one of the world's foremost hotels and conference venues, complete with 18-hole golf course and splendid dining facilities. Prior to the conversion, friends were invited to weekend demolition parties to smash down walls, rewire the electrics and rebuild the antiquated plumbing. The venture, once finished, was highly successful.

Lord Brocket married a model, Isa, and they had three children. But few realized that the marriage of this apparently rich and glamorous couple was soon falling apart, and Isa had become addicted to painkillers. Moreover, in the 1990s Brocket was facing financial disaster. Ten years earlier he had started buying classic Ferraris as an investment and, after they had increased their value tenfold in just a couple of years, his bank had funded him in the development of a business buying and selling vintage Ferraris. Unfortunately the classic car industry collapsed virtually overnight and the bank reclaimed its loan, eventually planning to seize Brocket Hall.

Faced with losing his family home, Lord Brocket made what he later described as the most foolish decision of his life. He, his wife and two mechanics arranged to have four valuable Ferraris dismantled, then they buried the parts and pretended they had been stolen, subsequently putting in an insurance claim for £4.5 million. Brocket would never actually collect any of the insurance money, as the bank came up with a rescue package, upon which the insurance claim was withdrawn. However, by a twist of fate, Isa Brocket was arrested for forging drug prescriptions, at which point she spilled the beans concerning the earlier insurance plot. Brocket was arrested and imprisoned for conspiracy to defraud, serving two and a half years in seven different prisons.

Lord Brocket still owns the Hall, which is now worth an estimated £42 million. It is rented out on a long-term lease to the CGA group, headed by chairman Dieter Klostermann. The group is now transforming the Hall into an exclusive residents' club, allowing its members to spend a certain amount of time there each year and to enjoy all the facilities, which now include a second golf course, a Michelin-starred restaurant and a spa, in exchange for an annual membership fee – all without having to worry about the burdens of real-estate ownership. Today Brocket Hall continues to attract well-known visitors, from Baroness Thatcher, who spent time there working on her memoirs, to Fergie, lead singer of The Black Eyed Peas, who recently shot the video for her debut single at the Hall. Lord Brocket now lives in London, works as an architect, has written his autobiography and has appeared on the British TV show 'I'm A Celebrity … Get Me Out Of Here'.

So what is the right size? Lord Brocket is not the only one who has struggled with an estate that was once an asset but has turned, in modern times, into a liability. A German prince whose family date back to the eleventh century once approached the director of a prestigious real-estate company with the intention of selling one of his family's castles. Although the family were one of the few that had managed to hold onto a good deal of the impressive wealth they had accumulated over the centuries, it had been decided to sell the castle to inject some ready cash into the princely household.

When presenting the property to the company director, the prince explained that the castle had always been in the family and thus was coming onto the open market for the first time in 580 years. This, he reasoned, together with his illustrious name and the 2,400 square metres (over 25,000 sq. ft) of living space and 500 hectares (1,235 acres) of grounds, must surely make for a highly desirable gem and a sales price in the ten digits.

Well, not quite. Although his reasoning was to some extent quite logical, it was also true that his family had not lived in the castle for over 65 years. As a result – apart from the medieval banquet hall, private chapel and wide selection of vast reception rooms – the property offered future owners no fewer than fifty (damp) bedrooms to choose from, a mere two completely out-dated bathrooms and a kitchen well suited to roasting a whole ox but not to boiling a morning egg. And while working wood-burning fireplaces in every room are usually an attractive asset in a luxury home, they are by no means a substitute for a modern central heating system, which turned out to be non-existent as well. So, rather than being a gem on the property market, the castle turned out to be more of a 'white elephant', with only very few potential purchasers likely to be willing to take on such a responsibility.

Lifestyles have also changed in modern times, making maintenance an issue. Until World War II it was not unusual for a moderately sized mansion, such as Cliveden in England, to have an indoor staff of twenty and an outdoor staff of the same size, while in a ducal house such as Chatsworth the numbers could be even higher. In the great houses of Italy, France or Germany, moreover, the number of retainers was often even greater than in England. As outlined earlier (see p. 13), most European mansions were also the hub of vast estates, which contained not only numerous outbuildings and significant holdings of agricultural land but often entire villages and churches as well. In England, large estates such as Woburn Abbey had several villages attached. Since most of these estates have now been broken up, only the great houses remain, with some surrounding ornamental land but without the revenue-generating agricultural operations. This, in turn, raises the question of how to maintain a property without selling it, turning it into a hotel or conference facility, or dismantling one's collection of vintage Ferraris.

The most sought-after size for the living space of a luxury home today is roughly between 300 and 800 square metres (3,250–8,500 sq. ft). A good number of newly built residences in the US offer well over 1,000 square metres (10,750 sq. ft), but these are usually the properties of billionaires and are only seldom found in the Old World. Up to 800 square metres will usually allow the owner to maintain a property with comparably manageable resources, such as a couple of housekeepers and cleaning ladies. The same applies with regard to structural maintenance. Features such as façades, roofs and windows are unlikely to require larger investments than the actual value of the property merits.

Once the property surpasses the threshold of 800 square metres, the situation tends to change. Both the daily and the long-term maintenance of a mansion with approximately 800 to 2,000+ square metres (8,500–21,500 sq. ft) of living area can quickly turn into a financial nightmare, even for the most hard-boiled property owner. Just imagine dusting and vacuuming fifty bedrooms every day, not to mention heating them....

Equal considerations apply to the size of a property's grounds. Most luxury properties will come with between 3,000 and 10,000 square metres (32,000–107,500 sq. ft) of land. Grounds of this size are usually relatively easy to maintain with the help of one full-time or perhaps a couple of part-time gardeners.

Some large estates, however, have grounds of anywhere between 10 and 500 hectares (25–1,235 acres). Needless to say, these require a drastically different budget to a mere ornamental garden of 1/500th the size. And in only the rarest of cases will lawn-mowing be the only maintenance issue for such an out-sized property; it is more likely that a château on grounds of 20 hectares (50 acres) will also have features such as formal French gardens, an ornamental lake and its own forest. While the idea of possessing one's own lake or woods may sound tempting, and may even promise the possibility of additional income through forestry, fishing and so on, these also require highly specialized maintenance. Lake maintenance, for example, can involve dredging, cladding, planting, weeding and algae control, and a comprehensive dredging operation alone can easily cost €100,000, and even go into the millions if structural works are necessary. Similarly, a forest comes with maintenance costs – for a professional forester, specialist equipment, and so on. And when one considers that one hectare of mixed forest will usually generate an income of perhaps €500 per year, the notion of potential side-revenue rapidly dwindles.

It is vitally important therefore to find the right balance when acquiring a luxury property. For a lucky few there will be no need to compromise on size, location, amenity, quality or lifestyle. These fortunate buyers will be able to create the property of their dreams.

The Downtown Loft

TRIBECA New York, USA

This five-storey penthouse in the heart of TriBeCa is undoubtedly one of the most stunning dwellings the quarter has to offer – and TriBeCa ('Triangle Below Canal Street') is one of the most *sought-after* neighbourhoods in downtown Manhattan. Like other downtown neighbourhoods, it was once an industrial district dominated by warehouses, but has now developed into an *exclusive* and expensive real-estate market, its streets lined with high-end boutiques and restaurants. Many residents work in the fashion and movie industries, and the area itself often serves as a location for movie and TV shoots. This *'townhouse in the sky'*, with its enormous windows and multiple terraces, pays homage to the area's industrial roots, offering an impression of *light and space* that is a rare find anywhere in Manhattan.

ABOVE Huge, sun-flooded spaces – spread out over two floors – are a reminder of the industrial roots of the neighbourhood. Here the double-height dining room is awash with light in the day and offers spectacular city views at night. It is also the perfect forum for bold works of art and interior furnishings, such as this Dale Chihuly chandelier.

ABOVE The loft boasts four terraces, all easy to maintain with trim hedges, box shrubs and seasonal flowers in planters. The rooftop doors open onto a fully equipped home gym.

RIGHT No mere penthouse, this extraordinary residence is a veritable townhouse sitting on top of a traditional red-brick downtown building. Doorman service is one of many added extras.

ABOVE This glamorous bathroom – complete with enormous stainless-steel bath – is en suite to the master suite, which stretches over a full floor and includes every amenity, from a fireplace to a separate jacuzzi room to a large sunset terrace.

RIGHT The custom-made library offers generous amounts of space for browsing and studying. Wood panelling lines the room, with polished brass fixtures and fittings.

OPPOSITE The grandiose height of the apartment is impressive. A stainless-steel and glass staircase connects the floors. There is also a private elevator.

Relaxed Island Living

FARSIDE Abaco, Bahamas

For the past two hundred years
the *Bahamas*, an archipelago
consisting of some two thousand cays
and seven hundred islands in the
Atlantic Ocean, have been synonymous
with *tropical island living*.
European influence dates back to
none other than Christopher Columbus,
whose first landfall in the New World was
on San Salvador Island, in the south.
Abaco lies in the north and
has enjoyed a colourful history.
Its earliest settlers were Loyalists fleeing
the American Revolution with their slaves.
The Bahamas later became a British
crown colony, but gained independence
in 1973. Today Abaco is a *welcoming*
haven of resorts and marinas —
and undoubtedly the most desirable
property on the main island is Farside.
Located on Tilloo Cay, minutes from
Elbow Cay and Marsh Harbour, Farside
benefits from beautiful living spaces and
a *peacefully relaxed* ambience.

ABOVE The property comprises one hectare (nearly 3 acres) of beautifully landscaped grounds. No fewer than twenty-four pairs of French doors surround the main living quarters and open onto the wide verandas that encircle the house.

RIGHT The large kitchen is ideally set up for preparing almost any kind of food or drink one could wish for. It has a commercial barbecue system and pizza oven, and the bar even contains a commercial soft-drinks dispenser.

OPPOSITE The main living area gets its relaxed atmosphere from an eclectic mix of antiques and furnishings, as well as unusual features like the fireplace made of coral and the mahogany baby grand piano in the background.

Relaxed Island Living

BELOW The bedrooms are all located off the main building, as is customary in traditional Caribbean design. Wooden French doors can be fully opened up for light and sea breeze, as well as incredible views.

OPPOSITE The dining room, open to the rafters, continues the inside/outside living theme. With its cool floor-tiles and multiple windows, including stained-glass detailing, it is an airy and informal space.

RIGHT The cobalt blue, free-form swimming pool is cut into solid limestone. On the south side of the property is an area of deep water; on the north side a serene bay.

BELOW In addition to the castle-like tower, the property contains a separate house with master bedroom, a guesthouse, a workshop and a hangar for the sea plane of the lucky owner. It also has a large dock with its own electric fuel pump and mooring space for several boats.

1001 Nights Dream

LAS BRISAS Marbella, Spain

Some properties bedazzle their visitors from the second they enter the front doors. This is one of them. Inspired by Indian and Moorish architecture, it is what dreams of 1,001 nights are made of. The spectacular palace of Las Brisas, however, is not located in India, or the Middle East, or an *exotic* island; rather, it can be found in the golf valley of Nueva Andalucia, in the European jet-set resort of Marbella. Onyx inlaid floors, hand-painted murals and precious mosaic tiles create an ambience that can only be described as *lavish*. The main residence features several spectacular reception rooms with vaulted ceilings, a formal dining room with fireplace, covered terraces, and three guest suites with their own sitting rooms. With a total living space of 1,500 square metres (16,000 sq. ft), this *unique estate* offers ample room to entertain and live well.

ABOVE The Indian and Moorish inspirations behind the architecture are plain to see in this view of the main house. Other features in the Oriental tradition include a central courtyard and vast rooftop terrace, providing panoramic views of La Concha and the coastline. Further aspects of the grounds – several lagoons, an enclosed bird sanctuary and an outdoor bar area – reflect the eclectic interior.

OPPOSITE BELOW The master suite boasts large proportions but retains a romantic and intimate atmosphere. It also features a dressing room and en-suite bathroom with jacuzzi, shower and steam room.

ABOVE The bathroom, with its unusual raised bath and curved window-surround, is a glamorous but comfortable space. Marble floors and matching walls combine with soft furnishings and fabrics to create an atmosphere of luxurious calm.

ABOVE The main reception room opens onto the dining room. Cleverly designed with a lowered ceiling for intimacy, it offers ample space for cosy dinners. Through the window can be seen the lush, tropically planted grounds.

RIGHT The vaulted ceiling of the main reception room is 10 metres (32 ft) high and has been hand-painted. The vastness of the living space allows for an intimate, informal seating arrangement as well as more traditional formal seating. The Arabian theme is also visible in the carved architraves and window designs.

Whenever the stress of managing one's home becomes too great, one tends to dream of living in a *hotel*. Twenty-four-hour room service, maid service, a friendly concierge to take care of life's little problems with a smile…. Would there be a better place to live out that dream than the *legendary* Pierre Hotel in New York? A city landmark, located on Fifth Avenue and 61st Street, the 41-storey Pierre was designed by the *New York* firm of Schultze and Weaver, and opened its doors in 1930 under the management of Charles Pierre Casalasco. Since 1959 the Pierre has been owned by a housing co-op of 76 owners, 30 of whom *live permanently* on the premises, among the hotel's 201 guest rooms. With stunning amenities and views over Central Park, an apartment in the Pierre offers a truly *five-star* experience.

OPPOSITE ABOVE AND BELOW Two of the nine rooms in the apartment are the formal dining room and the bright white kitchen. The apartment also includes a gracious octagonal gallery, an enormous master-bedroom suite with his-and-her dressing rooms and baths, two additional bedrooms and baths, as well as a separate guest apartment on the same floor.

ABOVE Rooms on a grand scale and a classic layout define the apartment. Fabulous views of the skyline are also a constant reminder of a location at the heart of one of the greatest cities in the world.

5

Provençal Paradise

LA MOUGINE Mougins, France

This beautiful Provençal estate offers the best of two worlds. While the Côte d'Azur features some of the mildest weather Europe has to offer, it also has a lot of high-density building and corresponding crowding; and while Provence is legendary for its *rural charm* and untouched countryside, it also surprises visitors with its strong winds, especially in winter. The lovely property of La Mougine manages to combine the Côte's weather and the allure of Provence. *Village life* is only a short walk away, in the form of Pablo Picasso's beloved Mougins, yet one is but minutes from the bustle of the Côte d'Azur. At the same time the house offers almost 1,000 square metres (some 10,500 sq. ft) of living space, including a majestic entrance hall, a library and a study, as well as a self-contained guest apartment and two staff apartments. This *country idyll* is just the place for living the good life.

OPPOSITE The extensive grounds – approximately 2.5 hectares (6.5 acres) – encompass terraced gardens and olive groves, as well as a swimming pool and pool house, tennis court and pétanque pitch. A substantial 350-square-metre (3,750 sq. ft) house also sits in the grounds, as well as a former chapel converted into a guesthouse.

BELOW The enclosed loggia, with its ample shaded seating, is the perfect place for a game of dominoes or a lazy lunch on a balmy afternoon. The property also contains a formal dining room and reception room.

LEFT The huge, well-appointed, rustic-style kitchen has vast catering capacity but also invites cosy meals in front of its own fireplace, in true Provençal style.

RIGHT On the grounds of the estate is a separate artist's studio. Thoughtfully designed with a mezzanine level, this space is filled with natural light.

BELOW The large fireplace and vibrant artworks lend a welcoming atmosphere to the high-ceilinged reception room, and carefully selected contemporary furniture creates a refreshing contrast.

6

Traditional Island Living

WEATHERSIDE Nassau, Bahamas

Nassau, the capital of the Bahamas, was founded by British settlers on New Providence Island. For decades the island was notorious as a 'pirate's republic'. Charming characters, including the legendary Blackbeard, were said to have made it their favourite haunt. Centuries later it has become the favourite haunt of *international* high society. Not only is New Providence blessed with stunning flora and fauna, it also benefits from a friendly local tax regime, as well as convenient proximity to the US (Miami is only a 45-minute flight away). Lyford Cay, located on the western tip of the island, is a particularly *sought-after enclave* – and the property of Weatherside, built in the 1970s as a winter retreat for a member of the renowned Mellon family of Philadelphia, is one of the most *upscale* homes in the Cay.

ABOVE The two bedroom suites in the pool guesthouse are in addition to the three bedroom suites in the main house, three more in the garden guesthouse, and two more in the gatehouse. Amenities-wise, the owners lack for nothing: the property also comes with two golf carts, a 5.5-metre (18 ft) Boston Whaler and a Chevrolet Trailblazer.

RIGHT Situated on top of a ridge, the property encompasses just under a hectare (around 2 acres) of manicured grounds, leading down to 60 metres (almost 200 ft) of prime, white-sand beachfront.

ABOVE With ten bedrooms and eleven bathrooms on some 1,115 square metres (12,000 sq. ft), this estate offers ample living – and dreaming – space. Pocket doors that slide into the walls add to the expansive indoor-outdoor ambience.

OPPOSITE AND ABOVE The beautifully appointed drawing room, filled with important antiques and artworks, provides stunning views of both the Atlantic Ocean and the Clifton Bay area.

Large, sheltered verandas extend both living and dining space. Apart from facilitating the view, the property's elevated position also allows balmy breezes to circulate.

7

A Grand London Residence

HYDE PARK GARDENS London, England

This majestic residence is one
of the most desirable properties in London.
As square-foot prices in the city have
rocketed stratospherically, and
a constant influx of super-rich
investors have brought with them
international money, important and
generously sized properties in the capital
have become an increasingly
rare commodity. Whereas a
City banker, barrister or Harley Street
doctor once took it for granted that
they would be able to live in the
right area in a decently sized
apartment or townhouse, many such
properties have become out of reach,
even for the privileged,
and prices once paid for entire blocks
now seem to be paid for single houses.
With a superb location and
splendidly proportioned quarters,
this Hyde Park maisonette exerts
a *sophisticated appeal*
and is a rare find indeed.

A Grand London Residence

ABOVE AND OPPOSITE A total of 16 generously proportioned rooms offer some 870 square metres (9,300 sq. ft) of living space. The apartment is laid out mainly over the raised ground and first floors.

RIGHT The apartment is located in this impressive, early nineteenth-century building on the north side of Hyde Park. It has its own entrance, private garden leading onto communal gardens, large private terrace, separate mews house with staff quarters (which in itself would make a highly desirable London property), and garage parking for up to four cars.

The Moroccan Oasis

BLED TARGUI Marrakech, Morocco

Marrakech, close to the Atlas mountains in southwest Morocco, has a thousand-year history and an almost mystical ring to it. But it first appeared on the radar of international high society in the 1960s and '70s, when a whole string of *celebrities* discovered it for themselves. Lord Lichfield's celebrated photograph of Talitha Getty, wife of John Paul Getty, crouched on a Marrakech rooftop, is probably the most famous legacy of the time. One fabled property that has seen its fair share of *illustrious* guests, from the Rolling Stones to European royalty, is Bled Targui — second home of Henriette von Bohlen und Halbach for more than thirty years. This green jewel, on the outskirts of Marrakech, is an *extraordinary* oasis that has attracted — and continues to attract — the rich and beautiful from all around the world.

The Moroccan Oasis

BELOW In the 1970s Henriette's husband Arndt von Bohlen und Halbach, the last heir to the Krupp steel fortune, had the Bled Targui residence built to his own specifications (see also p. 191 for more history). The lush gardens are spread over 1.5 hectares (4 acres).

OPPOSITE Very few changes have been made to the original décor. Every nook and cranny still breathes the magic atmosphere of a bygone era, while offering a truly Moroccan experience.

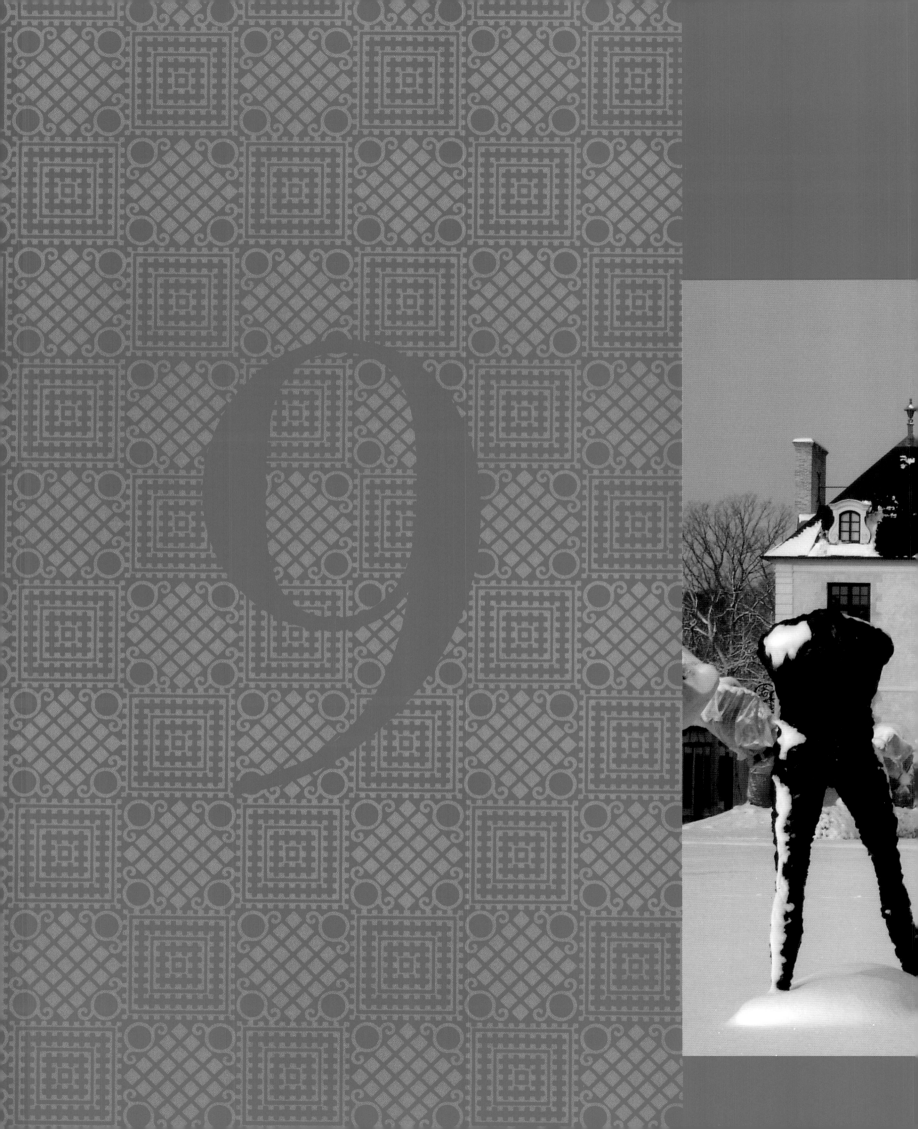

The French Château Revisited

LE COUDRECEAU   Orleans, France

Le Coudreceau is not your typical
French château. Originally built in the
17th and 18th centuries in classical style,
it has been completely *transformed*
according to the vision of one remarkable man.
Dominique Mandonnaud, after founding
the worldwide cosmetics empire Séphora,
and eventually selling it to
Bernard Arnault of the world's largest
luxury goods group LVMH, assembled
a dream-team of specialists to turn
Le Coudreceau into a *contemporary*,
21st-century estate, while maintaining
its ancient heritage. Jacques Moulin,
chief architect of France's historical
monuments, was put in charge of
the *historic* aspects of the renovation;
Thierry Despont, New York-based
interior designer for clients such as
Bill Gates and Calvin Klein,
was responsible for the interiors;
designer Philippe Kaufmann assisted
Mandonnaud in making his ideas concrete;
landscape designer Joseph Anguza
created the stunning grounds.
The result is *exceptional*.

RIGHT The renovation and restoration of Le Coudreceau lasted three intense years, but the perfectionism can be appreciated today. Exquisitely lit wooden beams soar over carefully chosen contemporary furniture and antique stone floors.

OPPOSITE The owner, himself a gifted sculptor and painter, has filled his home with stunning works of art. More artworks populate the grounds of more than 500 hectares (1,235 acres), with their ancient forests, picturesque ruins and lakes complete with islands.

BELOW The traditional and the contemporary co-exist: state-of-the-art facilities include underfloor heating, and built-in lighting and sound systems.

The Neo-Palladian Villa

VALLE DEL SOL Marbella, Spain

This impressive villa
near Marbella in Spain, is a fine
example of the Palladian style.
Italian Andrea Palladio, though he
lived over four hundred years ago,
is still widely considered the
most influential person in the
history of Western architecture.
Not only were earlier generations,
from Sir Christopher Wren to
Lord Burlington, inspired by his *style*,
even today important residences
are still being built
according to his principles.
This *Neo-classical* property
was constructed not in the
late 16th century but in 2004.
Its design faithfully reflects the
centuries-old typical Palladian villa
configuration – a dominant central focal
element flanked by servant wings –
but its spectacular amenities
could hardly be more
up to date.

ABOVE The gleaming, state-of-the-art kitchen provides every professional amenity for the many occupants the estate can house. As might be expected, the property also has its own wine bar and cellar.

OPPOSITE AND ABOVE Set in extensive gated grounds near the Guadalmina Golf Course, the property features practically every possible sporting amenity: an indoor heated swimming pool and whirlpool, a professional gym, a snooker room, a relaxation room, a sauna, a Turkish bath, and an Olympic-sized outdoor saltwater swimming pool and whirlpool.

ABOVE The outdoor pool, with its Classical-style architectural features, is the ideal spot for sunbathing or resting in the shade of the perfectly positioned palm trees.

ABOVE AND BELOW The extensive grounds encompass manicured formal gardens, huge terraces measuring over 550 square metres (5,900 sq. ft), pavilions, a riding area and horse boxes, as well as a floodlit tennis court. Water features also abound, from fountains and ponds to a lake with its own island.

The English Country House

BROCKET HALL Hertfordshire, England

Brocket Hall is one of those English *country houses* whose history would provide ample material for more than one film. Built around 1760 in the Georgian style, it is a house that has seen its fair share of *distinguished* inhabitants and visitors, from members of the royal family to several prime ministers. Its superb Neo-classical architecture and parkland setting, complete with Neo-Palladian bridge, are more than matched by the *stately* interiors. Antique furnishings abound, and there is also a noteworthy art collection that includes a Reynolds given by the Prince Regent, later King George IV, to his mistress, who happened to be the lady of the house. The painting can be admired in the ballroom today. This *magnificent* estate breathes history through every pore.

RIGHT On the walls of the billiard room can be found an exceptional collection of hunting trophies as well as portraits of several prime ministers. Rumour has it that Lord Palmerston, who married into the owner's family and himself became Prime Minister in 1855, expired on the billiard table, in the arms of a chambermaid....

ABOVE The drawing room, with portraits by De Lazlo and ceilings by Cipriani, also has outstanding antique furnishings and wall panelling.

RIGHT The house, designed in around 1760 by the architect James Paine for Sir Mathew Lamb, stands on the site of two predecessors, the first of which dates back to 1239.

OPPOSITE The Prince Regent, later George IV, was a frequent visitor to Brocket Hall and had his own suite there. In 1784 he had his sumptuously appointed bedroom specially decorated with hand-painted Chinese wallpaper.

LEFT This bathroom also has hand-painted walls, as well as traditional-style fittings in the form of a freestanding bath and 'throne'.

BELOW The spacious and airy Lady Melbourne Suite offers panoramic views over the Georgian parkland, the Broadwater Lake and James Paine's Neo-Palladian bridge.

A Palace in an Apartment

MIDTOWN EAST New York, USA

Living in Manhattan often means
living in an *apartment*, as
freestanding houses are virtually non-existent,
and even terraced townhouses are rare.
What better solution to the
problem than to create a *palace*
within an apartment?
Oscar-winning producer Marty Richards
and his late wife, Johnson & Johnson
heiress Mary Lea Johnson Richards,
originally purchased this stunning
14-room duplex because they were
impressed with the building's
high level of security and
impeccable service, but, after that,
they decided to spare no expense
in creating *the ultimate* in
luxurious living and entertaining.
The apartment, designed and renovated
by renowned decorator Tony Ingrao,
now offers an *unparalleled*
Neo-classical environment, with gold-covered
mouldings, over 3-metre-high (11 ft) ceilings,
hardwood *parquet de Versailles* floors,
and wood panelling imported from
an 18th-century French château.
The residence is now one of the
finest in New York City.

A Palace in an Apartment

BELOW The phenomenal – and truly palatial – master bathroom is the owner's favourite room. It features an exact copy of Napoleon's tent, painted on glass – a feature that can perhaps best be enjoyed while listening to the built-in music system that runs throughout the entire property.

ABOVE The apartment boasts trompe-l'œil hand-painted walls and antique marble fireplaces throughout. Stunning views of the East River are an added extra.

ABOVE The apartment is ideal for entertaining – and, from Henry Kissinger to JFK, from Michael Bolton to the Village People, it has seen plenty of notable guests.

13

The Spanish Colonial Mansion

PALM BEACH Florida, USA

This mansion is one of
the most important historic
oceanfront estates in Palm Beach –
a community that is not exactly
lacking in superlative properties.
The house was originally designed
by the architect Julius Jacobs
for the E. Z. Nutting family
in 1926, during the early years
of Palm Beach's ascent to
high-society haven.
A perfect example of the
Spanish Colonial style,
with elements of Mediterranean style,
the property has recently been brought
back to its former glory by renowned
preservationist Bill Elias.
Spread over 2,260 square metres
(24,300 sq. ft), and on four levels, the
mansion offers ample living space
for even the most *discerning*
owner, be it in 1926 or the
new millennium.

ABOVE In addition to the tennis court and large pool, this property features an extremely rare commodity – a deeded beach parcel.

LEFT Artfully crafted ceiling beams are exposed, and the fireplaces and door ornaments are handcarved in stone.

ABOVE As part of the renovation works, technologically advanced impact-glass windows have been installed and now protect inhabitants against the forces of nature that so often make themselves felt in Florida.

The Perfect Pied-à-Terre

EATON PLACE London, England

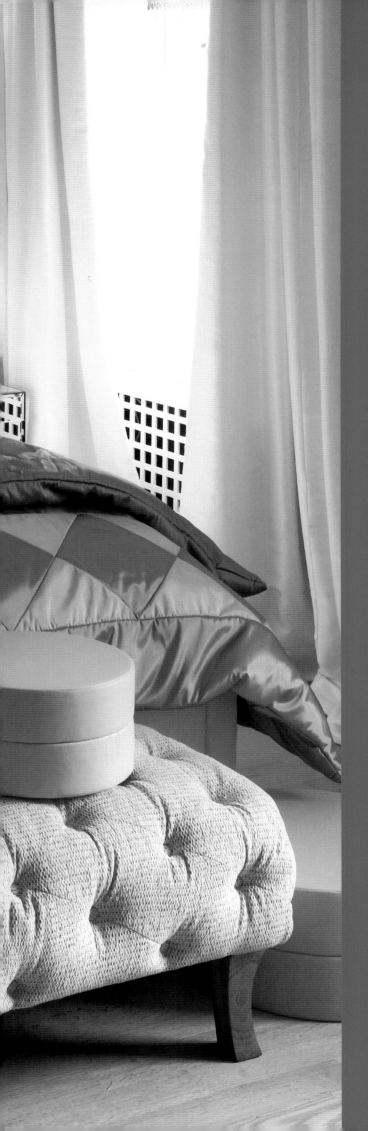

The French expression *pied-à-terre* literally means 'foot on the ground', and usually designates a secondary home in one of the world's great cities, such as London, Paris or Rome. Such residences tend to be seen as a more *personal* alternative to anonymous hotel rooms by those members of international high society who are 'not too badly off' and can afford a bolthole in the metropolises they frequent. A classic pied-à-terre – like this one in one of the best parts of the highly sought-after Belgravia – is situated in a *prime location*, with the owner's favourite spots right on the doorstep. Such properties also tend not be too large, in order to keep maintenance in between visits to a *minimum* for perfect city living. Nonetheless, what a pied-à-terre lacks in size, it often makes up for in décor.

THIS PAGE Located on the first floor, this pied-à-terre features wonderfully proportioned rooms and plenty of stylish details, as well as high-quality features like a south-facing balcony and direct elevator access.

OPPOSITE The property was elegantly refurbished by Essenza Style. Décor is particularly important in a small space. Indeed, some bills presented by well-known international interior designers for the decoration of fashionable pied-à-terres can equal the price of a nice family home in the suburbs….

15

A Seaside Penthouse

HEILIGENDAMM Baltic Coast, Germany

The German *seaside resort* of
Heiligendamm is today a secret tip
among the international *beau monde*
– but this hasn't always been the case.
Founded in 1793 by the Grand Duke of
Mecklenburg, it developed in the
19th century into a favourite meeting place
of Europe's upper classes, holding its own
against other *fashionable* resorts
such as Deauville and Biarritz.
However, its fortunes steadily declined
during the 20th century. After many
ill-fated ownership changes, it became
an East German state-owned property following
World War II. Then, after German reunification,
its deteriorated *historic* centre
was acquired by real-estate entrepreneur
Anno August Jagdfeld's Fundus group.
Jagdfeld, together with his wife, style arbiter
Anne Maria, revived Heiligendamm.
Its white classicist buildings – including
the 'Burg Hohenzollern' – were
restored to their former glory, and today
the resort is once again a luxurious,
highly *elegant*, yet understated
destination.

ABOVE AND RIGHT This penthouse apartment is the private pied-à-terre of Anne Maria Jagdfeld, and offers an eclectic mix of classic furniture and furnishings, contemporary Chinese art and timeless materials. Jagdfeld's previous developments have included such bastions of good taste as the luxury-goods emporium Quartier 206 and the China Club in Berlin. Her husband, Anno August Jagdfeld, is perhaps best known for resurrecting Berlin's fabled Grand Hotel Adlon, which – just like Heiligendamm – had once been a magnet for international high society but had fallen into a post-war decline.

OPPOSITE Sea air and sea views have enticed visitors ranging from Russian Grand Duchess Maria Alexandrova and the German Kaiser in the nineteenth century to the top-ranking politicians who worked – and relaxed – in the special atmosphere of Heiligendamm during the 2007 G8 summit.

The Frank Lloyd Wright Icon

LOVNESS ESTATE Stillwater, Minnesota, USA

Frank Lloyd Wright is often called 'the greatest American architect of all time'. So how did a young couple with limited financial means end up with an *iconic estate* designed by such an eminent figure? The answer is: courage, determination and a lot of hard work. In the early 1950s, Don Lovness, a young engineer, and his wife Virginia had purchased a plot of *prime property* in Stillwater, Minnesota. In 1954, Virginia managed to obtain an appointment with Wright to show him her designs for a studio. Wright, by then already in his 80s, quickly made so many changes that little remained of her original plan. The upside, however, was that he agreed personally to *design* a studio for her. Armed with his original plans, Virginia, Don and their two small daughters moved into a trailer and began to build their dream property stone by stone. Today it is a *masterpiece* of modern architecture.

ABOVE Though he never visited it, due to illness, the estate is just as Frank Lloyd Wright intended – a natural reorganization of the landscape's own materials, stone and wood.

OPPOSITE The Studio – based on a variation of Wright's 'Usonian' houses – makes the most of its prime 8-hectare (20-acre) plot overlooking White Bear Lake.

OPPOSITE AND BELOW All the interior furniture was designed by Wright, who advised and offered guidance throughout the project. The Lovnesses also travelled often to his fabled studio, Taliesin, to give updates and consult the master.

ABOVE The estate comprises the Studio – a 170-square-metre (1,800 sq. ft) home, complete with master suite, children's wing and spacious living room overlooking the lake – and a second house, the Cottage, built a few years later.

17

A Fairytale Castle

CHÂTEAU D'AIGUEFONDE Midi-Pyrénées, France

Describing Château d'Aiguefonde simply
as a place rich with history would
be quite an understatement. Although
the *château* in its current form dates back
to the 16th and 18th centuries,
its earliest foundations can be traced
back more than two thousand years, to when
the Romans erected a watchtower on the site.
The château is located in the Pays Cathare,
an extremely *picturesque* part of the
Languedoc region in southern France.
Over the centuries, the château's
inhabitants were more than once
caught up in the region's notorious
conflicts between Catholics and the
reformist Cathars, and witnessed such events
as the château's plundering by Catholic
troops, a royal visit by King Henry IV
and a murder. In our more peaceful
times, the château has been lovingly
restored by Dutch artist Paul de Vilder,
who stumbled across it, and its fountains,
waterfalls and overgrown Le Nôtre gardens,
and decided to revive the
enchanting sleeping beauty.

OPPOSITE AND ABOVE   Owner Paul de Vilder worked as a five-star-hotel manager in New York, South America and Tokyo before changing careers and becoming an accomplished painter. It was he who brought the château back to its former glory by painstakingly restoring it and carefully adding period antiques, paintings and tapestries from the sixteenth, seventeenth and eighteenth centuries.

THIS PAGE AND OPPOSITE Modern amenities have been unobtrusively added to the château. It now has a large number of comfortable bedroom suites, a professional gourmet kitchen and a swimming pool, ensuring that life is a little more comfortable than in medieval times, though still with plenty of romance. From many of the windows there are stunning views of the magnificently restored grounds, including the English park with a *rivière à l'anglaise*, complete with waterfalls and basins, and a *rivière russe*, with a spectacular series of high fountains.

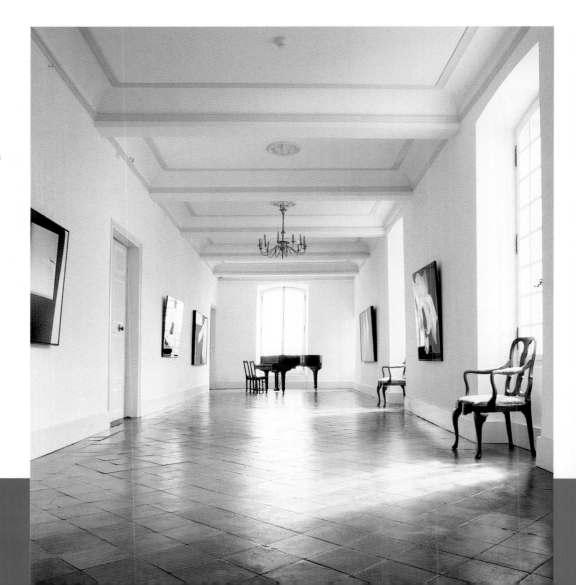

18

The Neutra Masterpiece

SINGLETON RESIDENCE Bel Air, California, USA

The Singleton Residence combines three
key ingredients that make for a truly
extraordinary property:
a legendary architect, a highly desirable
location, and an owner who enjoys
worldwide renown in his own right.
The architect: Richard Neutra.
The location: Bel Air, California.
The owner: haircare legend Vidal Sassoon.
Neutra, one of the founding fathers of
the 'California Modern Style', which has
enjoyed an unparalleled renaissance
since the 1990s and is nowadays once
again a *connoisseurs'* favourite,
was commissioned to create the
Singleton Residence in 1959 for
Henry Singleton, co-founder of electronics
giant Teledyne, and subsequently
one of the wealthiest men in the USA.
The property – now beautifully renovated
and extended by Sassoon – sits on top
of Bel Air, on more than 2 hectares
(5 acres), and offers *spectacular*
views over the Los Angeles area.

ABOVE AND OPPOSITE BELOW Richard Neutra designed the property to sit in perfect harmony with nature. Vidal Sassoon's comprehensive renovation has expanded the estate to meet today's living standards, while respecting the original spirit and integrity. The property now includes a sitting room/screening room, a spacious art gallery, two junior bedroom suites, and a large master wing incorporating a private sitting room, bedroom and bathroom including wet-room, as well as an adjoining additional suite/office/gym.

ABOVE: In addition to seamlessly adding to the property, including the new master bedroom wing and art gallery, Sassoon has expanded the original kitchen. It has beautiful views over the perfectly located swimming pool.

19

The Country Retreat

NORTHWOOD Long Island, New York, USA

Judging by its appearance, this fine country house should be somewhere in Normandy, France. The *peaceful haven* of Longwood, however, is located only a short car ride from New York City. Many city residents dream of a *country place*, but the question is: where? The Hamptons are a classic choice, but four-hour rides (residents always insist it's only two) from Manhattan to Southampton during the season are not overly tempting to the cash-rich and time-poor; Greenwich, Connecticut, offers *beautiful* scenery and perfect railroad connections, but is so expensive it has a density of billionaires bordering on the ridiculous. An interesting, though not necessarily cheap, alternative is Oyster Bay Cove in Nassau County. With a population of only 2,200, this village is a refreshingly *tranquil* contrast to the bustle of the city. A property like Northwood – with its original Tudor-style indoor tennis court, 12-stall stable and other outbuildings, is a city dweller's *dream*.

ABOVE Northwood looks like an advertisement for refined East Coast living. The current mansion with some 1,660 square metres (17,900 sq. ft) of living space was built in 1948 by John Schiff, replacing an earlier Tudor-style structure three times this size, built in 1906 by John's father, Mortimer Schiff.

RIGHT AND OPPOSITE
The ten bedrooms, fifteen fireplaces and ten bathrooms may look antique, but the mansion has only recently been renovated to offer all the amenities of the twenty-first century, including oil-heating, central air-conditioning, an elevator and a back-up generator for those stormy Long Island nights.

The Big One

PALM BEACH Florida, USA

What can one say about *Donald Trump*?
No book about luxury real estate would
be complete without a profile of
this extraordinary *personality*.
Born in 1946 in Queens, New York,
the son of a wealthy developer,
Donald graduated from the New York
Military Academy and the Wharton School
of Economics. Five years after joining
his father's *real-estate* company –
having 'flirted briefly with the idea of attending
film school' – he founded his own company,
and in the 1980s quickly became known
as a bullish investor. His residential
projects, such as Trump Tower,
became *landmarks*, and he branched
out his business activities. The real-estate
slump of the early 1990s, however,
left him saddled with colossal debts.
Unfazed, he restructured and
eventually emerged, once again, as a
billionaire. It is little wonder that
his palatial Palm Beach home is
anything but modest.

OPPOSITE AND BELOW The 2.5-hectare (6.5-acre) estate features over 170 metres (570 ft) of direct ocean frontage along with over 6,225 square metres (67,000 sq. ft) of living space. Sweeping sea views, broad Bermuda lawns and a 30-metre (100 ft) pool, together with a ballroom, a media room, a magnificent master suite, five guest suites, a wine bistro, an art gallery, a collector's basement, staff quarters and any amenity one can think of, make this property one of the most expensive in the world.

GUIDE TO BUYING A LUXURY PROPERTY

ESSENTIAL TIPS FOR THE LUXURY PROPERTY INVESTOR

LOCALITY

An apartment on New York's Upper East Side, a villa in Marbella, a romantic château in Burgundy: luxury real estate exists in many forms. As we have seen, such properties cater to many different needs and aspirations. Far from being a simple home, they are also a status symbol, an expression of one's personality and distinct taste, and, of course, a significant financial asset. However, when a luxury property is bought as a long-term investment, certain rules should be adhered to. The following sections give an overview of the many aspects to be considered when acquiring a luxury property.

'Location, location, location'

The above phrase seems to have been quoted in just about every real-estate publication of the last fifty years but, despite its ubiquity, it still rings true. After all, almost every aspect of a property can be changed apart from its location…. Thus, a property in only average condition in a prime spot will generally sell much better than a perfect, one-of-a-kind property in the middle of nowhere. For this reason so-called 'insider markets' in remote locations that are heralded as future hot, up-and-coming, real-estate territories should always be examined with a good dose of scepticism and common sense. As a rule, only time will tell whether a market has really been able to establish itself as a new prime location or whether it has only been the subject of a short-lived frenzy.

Marrakech first came under the international spotlight in the late 1960s, when such international jetsetters as the Gettys and the Krupp heir Arndt von Bohlen und Halbach and his wife Princess Henriette von Auersperg settled there. However, the city then faded from public consciousness and did not re-surface until the late 1990s. Since then, however, it has steadily gained momentum, and is currently once again a highly sought-after location for a luxury home. This trend has been supported and bolstered by the parallel development of high-end hotels, such as the local Amanresort, and quality real-estate projects in the vicinity.

Another example of a market that has been able to establish itself as a permanent fixture on the international luxury real-estate scene is the island of Mallorca. From the 1960s to the 1980s this Spanish territory was known amongst the upper classes as 'the island of cleaning-women' because it was a favourite holiday destination of the English and German working classes. However, its mild year-round climate, its easy accessibility from most European city centres and its natural beauty also attracted members of international high society, who started to invest in holiday homes there. This trend gained momentum, and Mallorca is now established as one of the most sought-after – and expensive – luxury home markets in Europe. Real-estate owners on Mallorca have included members of the Spanish royal family, tennis legend Boris Becker, supermodel Claudia Schiffer, and Hollywood legend Michael Douglas and his wife Catherine Zeta-Jones.

On the other hand, journalists and real-estate 'experts' have long predicted that the picturesque Italian region of Marken would see a real-estate boom similar to that of Tuscany in the 1990s. Their predictions have still to be fulfilled, and Marken today remains one of the quiet backwaters in Italian real estate.

Accessibility

So which factors are decisive for the fate of any real-estate market? One of the most important is, and always has been, accessibility. Even the most wonderful exotic paradise will never develop into a long-term, high-end, real-estate market if it can only be reached under the most difficult of circumstances.

It is, for example, quite possible nowadays to become the owner of an entire island. Specialized companies offer islands all over the world (the biggest choice can usually be found in the South Pacific or in Canada). Initially prices often seem surprisingly low, starting at well under half a million US dollars and often not costing more than $5 million. So where's the catch? Well, even the most alluring tropical haven will quickly lose its charm if it can only be reached via the most complicated, and consequently expensive, connections.

SAMPLE ITINERARY

1. Fly Zurich (ZRH) – London (LHR)
2. Change terminal: Terminal 2 – Terminal 3
3. Fly London (LHR) – LA (LAX)
4. Change terminal: Terminal 4 – Terminal B
5. Fly LA (LAX) – Papeete (PPT)
6. Fly Papeete (PPT) – Bora Bora (BOB)
7. Transfer by boat or helicopter Bora Bora – private island.

An example of tricky accessibility: how to get from Zurich to a private island near Bora Bora, part of the Society Islands archipelago in French Polynesia, located approximately 280 kilometres (175 miles) northwest of Tahiti

Newly established access facilities, on the other hand, can change the face of an entire region. The possibility of reaching a destination on a regular basis by such means as low-cost airlines or high-speed trains can trigger a real-estate boom. The island of Ibiza, for example, was for decades regarded as a hippie paradise that exerted no strong appeal on the *beau monde*. In the 1990s, however, it became more and more accessible via new flight connections and that suddenly made it an interesting location for a second luxury home for many Spaniards and other Europeans.

The Provence region in France has seen a similar development. Of course, it has always been a destination of choice, not only for the Impressionist painters at the turn of the century but for anyone in search of idyllic surroundings and a mild climate. From a real-estate standpoint, however, it only became really attractive once it became accessible via the French high-speed TGV train from Paris, and the airports in Marseilles and Avignon.

INFRASTRUCTURE

Another important factor that often determines the fate of a real-estate market – but one that also tends to be overlooked – is local infrastructure.

Social infrastructure

For many people one of the main attractions of a luxurious secondary residence is to 'get away from it all', but if getting away from it all means that the nearest butcher or supermarket is a 55-minute drive away, enthusiasm for the unspoilt countryside has been known quickly to wane. Bare necessities aside, if the next theatre, cinema or decent boutique is a two-hour drive away, this may quickly lead to considerable frustration levels for all but the most hardcore hermits. Local infrastructure with a sufficient supply of amenities and facilities is therefore paramount.

Medical infrastructure

An adequate medical infrastructure is of vital (in the true meaning of the word) importance. Curiously enough, this point often enters a purchaser's mind only when a medical emergency has arisen … and by then it may well be too late. One should always ensure that qualified medical assistance – i.e. a hospital or registered doctor – can be reached at a minimum within 60 to 90 minutes. If a patient has to be transported for longer than that, it can have serious consequences.

Property infrastructure

The only thing worse than having no social infrastructure is having no infrastructure at all. The purchase of an isolated property – such as an old farm, or cottage or, above all, an island – may have many advantages, but if the property is not equipped with the utilities we nowadays take for granted, such as plumbing, electricity and phone lines, the dream property can quickly turn into a nightmare.

Of course, the installation of such infrastructure is almost always possible. Water can be obtained by connecting to the local supply system, by drilling a well or, for seaside properties, by installing a desalination system. Similarly, electricity can nowadays be obtained through the local system or through stand-alone generators, be they fuel-, wind- or solar-powered. However, all these options can become very time- and money-consuming – not to mention the considerable investment in nerves.…

The existence of both a sufficient practical as well as social infrastructure is therefore usually a good indicator of the attractiveness of a property and its on-going real-estate market for future buyers.

LOCAL POLITICS AND ECONOMICS

The local political and economic landscape are additional factors that play a decisive role in determining the fate of a real-estate market. Of course, a buyer of a property might argue that they only want to use their luxury home as a retreat and have no intention of becoming involved in local politics or economics. Although this may be true, the proprietor will in many ways be dependent on the way the local political system and its economy functions.

Dubai, for example, is currently emerging as a marketplace that is re-positioning itself not only as a temporary holiday destination but also as a long-term, luxury real-estate market. Visionary projects such as The World and The Palms (see p. 17) have been designed to attract a permanent high-end clientele to the country. This, however, has only become possible through the recent establishment of a system of property ownership that has also abolished the legal barriers that once made it impossible for foreigners to acquire real estate in the country.

Other territories such as Sri Lanka, Bali and the Philippines are known today as world-class holiday destinations which are also attracting a regular and loyal clientele from the ranks of international high society.

Unfortunately, however, political upheavals on a national or regional scale – as well as prevalent cultures of political corruptness – can result in a wide range of unhappy surprises for homeowners in some areas. These can range from failure to obtain construction permits, at least without paying bribes to a number of officials, to the complete loss of a property due to political changes and consequent new laws and regulations. Such locations, however, have generally not yet evolved as established long-term, luxury real-estate markets.

It is almost always safest to invest in a property market that has been regarded as a high-end destination for some time. Despite any predictions to the contrary, the status of such markets as the French Riviera, or international hubs like London, New York and Paris, is unlikely to change on a permanent basis. Of course, strikes, inflated living costs and crime rates create headlines from time to time, but these are also unlikely to change the long-term prospects of such real-estate locations (see pp. 174–89 for an overview of the world's most established real-estate markets).

CONDITION

So what are the criteria to look out for once the decision has been made to purchase a luxury home in a particular market? One of the most important factors is, of course, the condition of the property. The acquisition of a recently renovated property may initially require a larger investment than for a property in a lesser condition, but in the long run this may turn out to be the smartest investment the buyer ever makes.

Apparently simple repair jobs in – at first glance – well-maintained properties can quickly develop into full-blown restoration works if basic installations such as central heating, electric wiring or plumbing have not been updated for some time. In particular, historic properties such as castles, mansions and châteaux can turn into financial, logistical and administrative headaches. In many countries, including France, England and Germany, a lot of properties of historical or architectural importance are classified as 'historical monuments' or similar (see below), and these classifications can drastically limit the owner's ability to effect major or even minor changes.

On the other hand, updating features such as bathrooms or kitchens can usually be done within a predictable and manageable budget if the basic structures are in good condition. A tricky point in the acquisition can be determining to what extent a buyer should pay for the taste of the previous owner, because many luxury homes have been decorated throughout by a particular interior designer in his or her signature style. Depending on the style and the reputation of the designer, the cost of this can run into the hundreds of thousands of dollars. On the other hand, many new owners will want to start re-decorating their new home immediately after purchase, as they not only have their own personal style but often also their own preferred interior designer whom they use for all their properties around the world. It is therefore quite often impossible to recuperate completely one's investment in the interior design of a property. Investments in more or less basic features, however, such as state-of-the-art heating or wiring systems, may to some degree be considered in the eventual sale price. Purely cosmetic features such as custom-made furniture, wall-coverings or window-dressings will only on the rarest of occasions be financially honoured by the buyer.

In case of doubt about the actual condition of a property, it is almost always a sound move to obtain independent advice from a specialist. Architects, chartered surveyors or independent appraisers, as well as building or restoration companies, can be retained to provide a professional assessment of a property's current condition and any possible investments needed for the future. The outlay in obtaining such advice may at first appear to be an unnecessary expenditure on top of the considerable other expenses resulting from the acquisition of a luxury property. However, when taking into consideration the enormous costs that – especially in the case of a historic property – can often be caused by works, and indeed can easily surpass the actual purchase price, this expense can quickly turn out to be an extremely wise investment.

Finally, it should not be forgotten that independent surveying expertise may also strengthen one's negotiating position when dealing with the seller, especially in cases where the specialist has discovered defects that may have been unknown to – or undisclosed by – the seller.

LEGAL CONSIDERATIONS

Similar considerations apply to the independent assessment of the legal parameters of a luxury property purchase.

Purchase restrictions

In countries such as the Philippines, Indonesia, Malaysia and other areas of the Pacific Ocean, foreigners are often not permitted to purchase real estate on a freehold basis. Other countries such as Switzerland, New Zealand and Australia restrict the access of non-resident foreign buyers to local real estate by establishing quotas and/or conditions for acquisition of property. The specific laws and regulations of each country should therefore be carefully checked when considering a purchase.

Protected historic properties

Historic properties are especially often subject to legal obligations and encumbrances. These can consist of restrictions and regulations as to how the substance of the property may be altered; they can also consist of encumbrances such as the obligation to make parts of the property accessible to the general public. In England, for example, certain properties of historic or architectural value are 'listed' by the government; in other words, corresponding to their historical importance, they are classified into different categories (Grade I, Grade II, etc.), which in turn defines what can be done with the property. Listing means that the entire property, i.e. the building, its interior and exterior as well as the area surrounding it, is protected. The owner of such a property is not allowed to change the character of the building, or to alter, demolish or extend it without permission (the so-called Listed Building Consent, or LBC). Thus, it is extremely important to check what works have been done by the previous owner, whether they required an LBC, whether consent was granted and the work carried out in accordance with the consent. While the new owner cannot be prosecuted for any previous unauthorized work, they may be forced to rectify it at their own expense. Similar regulations exist in almost all Western countries, including France (loi monuments historiques) and Germany (Denkmalschutz). The up-side of legally imposed restrictions and encumbrances, however, often consists in financial incentives given by the state, such as tax breaks or even government funding, for approved restoration projects.

Building permits

Another related legal aspect that is worth checking out is the adherence to or validity of past or existing construction permits, even if the property is not protected as a historic building. In many countries, extremely strict building ordinances tempt owners to exceed the limits of their approved construction permit once the building work has received official consent. What many purchasers do not realize is that a new owner – who may well have acquired an illegally constructed property in good faith – often remains liable for adherence to agreed building standards. In countries such as Spain and Italy, the proud owners of a new property may one day find a letter from the local government in the morning mail ordering them to demolish parts of their newly acquired villa (on the island of Mallorca, for example, even the most prominent of homeowners have not been immune to the – sometimes quite arbitrary – enforcement of such building regulations: tennis star Boris Becker was forced to change the plans for his new island estate several times). Consulting a local attorney, notary or specialized title company, then, is likely to be a smart investment for saving both time and money in the future.

Negotiations

Finally, an appropriate price should be paid for the luxury property. Unfortunately, buyers' and sellers' ideas of what constitutes an appropriate price often seem to differ to a marked degree. A good knowledge of the local real-estate market, however, will usually enable a potential buyer to negotiate much more efficiently. The internet, as well as local and national real-estate publications, are a quick and effective means of getting a good basic understanding of local markets.

However, especially in large-scale transactions of a more elaborate financial and logistical nature, a buyer will usually benefit immensely by procuring professional help right from the start. A qualified real-estate agent will not only considerably narrow down the sea of potential offerings by making a pinpointed pre-selection according to the buyer's criteria, but will also be able to negotiate effectively between buyer and seller thanks to their independent standing and in-depth knowledge of the local market.

Moreover, truly professional real-estate brokers will also act as a one-stop-shop for their clients, guiding them towards other trusted professionals, such as architects and lawyers. After the transaction has been completed, a high-end broker will continue to take care of his or her client, introducing them into the local community and giving useful recommendations for local staff, maintenance companies, interior designers, handymen, and so on.

TYPES OF LUXURY PROPERTY

There are of course dozens, if not hundreds, of different types of luxury real-estate property, designed in all sorts of architectural styles. Entire volumes could be – and indeed have been – written trying to describe and classify the variations.

Even the terms that are used to describe such properties differ widely. For example in England, the term 'country house' does not simply describe any property located in a rural area: on the contrary, it is usually used only for a distinctive building that was once the centrepiece of an agricultural estate large enough to provide the landowner with sufficient income to be accepted as a member of the aristocracy or gentry. This usually required an estate of at least 400 hectares (1,000 acres); a few proprietors owned more than a hundred times this minimum. A 'country house' like this would probably contain at least 20 rooms and 750 square metres (8,000 sq. ft) of living space. Most country houses also have large grounds comprised of a garden in the immediate vicinity of the house, plus a larger park beyond the garden which is grazed by animals but which also has aesthetic and recreational purposes. Many of the finest gardens in Britain are country-house gardens.

Confusingly enough, a 'country house', in the English sense of the word, can be built in any architectural style. More confusingly still, many different terms are used to designate a country house, including 'hall', 'castle', 'park', 'palace', 'court', 'abbey', 'priory', 'house' and 'grange'. Although the name may provide a clue as to the history of the house, it may also have been chosen purely on the whim of its owner. For example, many country houses that are called 'Castle [Something]' never had any defensive purpose whatsoever.

In most other countries, however, such large luxury homes will usually be referred to by more precise terms depending on their size, history, architectural style and function. Thus, a fortified building will usually be called a 'castle', an unfortified building with towers a 'château', and so on. What follows is a short but comprehensive overview of these and other sought-after property types on the luxury real-estate market.

CASTLE

A castle – from the Latin *castellum* – was a structure that was fortified for defence against an enemy and generally served as military headquarters dominating the surrounding countryside. The term is most often applied to a self-contained fortress, usually dating from the Middle Ages.

Originally, true castles were places of protection and retreat from invading enemies – a heritage visible in such features as portcullises, battlements, moats and drawbridges. However, castles were not only defensive, but also offensive weapons: especially during the High Middle Ages, many were built as bases for territorial expansion and strategic regional control. Eventually, they evolved into residences for the lord who built them.

In later times, the term 'castle' has been used for unfortified buildings as well. However, these should more properly be referred to as châteaux, manors, and so on.

CHÂTEAU (PALAIS)

A château is a grand country house without fortifications, usually located in a French-speaking region (a fortified château, i.e. a castle, is known in France as a 'château fort'). A true château will generally have some sort of tower, otherwise it is more likely to be designated a mansion or manor (see below). One location with an extraordinarily high density of châteaux is the Loire Valley, home to more than three hundred examples built between the tenth and twentieth centuries first by the French kings and then by the nobility.

The urban counterpart of the 'château', in Francophone regions, is the 'palais'. This usage is somewhat different from that of the term 'palace' in English, where it is usually reserved only for the grandest royal or aristocratic residences, such as Buckingham Palace or Blenheim Palace.

In German-speaking regions the equivalent of the château is the Schloss (a German fortified castle is known as a Burg).

MANSION
(MANOR, *MAISON DE MAÎTRE*)

The term 'mansion' or 'manor' – the root deriving from the Latin *manere*, to remain or to stay – usually describes a large stately dwelling in the country, though sometimes also in the city. Their lack of fortifications or towers generally distinguishes them from castles or châteaux. Again, however, there does not exist a uniform, foolproof definition, and the terms will be used differently from country to country.

The English word 'manse' originally defined a property large enough for the incumbent parish priest to support himself (like an Italian villa, see below), but in these modern times neither a mansion nor a villa is expected to be self-sustaining in this way.

VILLA

The term 'villa' originally referred to the dwelling of the ruling classes of the Roman Empire. In post-Roman times it came to mean a self-sufficient, usually fortified Italian or Gallo-Roman farmstead. The term was later used in some regions to designate not only such country estates, but also entire towns (such as Vila Real and Villadiego). In the Renaissance, 'villas' once more came to signify Italian country houses, such as Villa Borghese with its famous gardens, or the Villa Medici on the outskirts of Rome. The villas designed in the later sixteenth century in the Veneto region by Andrea Palladio (see below) have remained influential for over four hundred years.

The English, in the early eighteenth century, took up the term. Thanks to the many Palladio followers such as Inigo Jones, Neo-

Palladian villas soon dotted the English landscape. However, the real corruption of the term began in the nineteenth century, when it was extended to describe almost any suburban house that was free-standing in a landscaped plot, as opposed to a 'terrace' of joined houses. By the time 'semi-detached villas' were being constructed at the turn of the twentieth century, the term finally collapsed through overuse. In post-colonial Britain, after the First World War, the so-called suburban 'villa' became a simple bungalow.

The term 'villa' is therefore rarely used in the luxury real-estate business in the UK, nor in the US. However, in other parts of the world, the concept is alive and well. In Western and Southern European countries it is used to refer to a single-family house of a certain size, which does not qualify as a more significant dwelling such as a château, mansion, manor, etc., but is larger and/or more distinctive than a simple 'house'.

Palladian (-style) villa

A Palladian villa is one of the noblest structures in existence, and has nothing in common with its poor suburban English cousin. The Italian architect Andrea Palladio (1508–1580) can probably be considered the most influential person in the history of Western architecture.

Palladio started out in the field of stonemasonry, but in 1537 met his future mentor and benefactor Count Gian Giorgio Trissino, one of the period's leading scholars. Trissino introduced Palladio to the principles of classical architecture and other disciplines of Renaissance education, and opened the door for him to a growing circle of patrons. By 1538 Palladio had begun construction of Villa Godi, the first of a series of country villas and urban palaces designed for noble patrons in the Vicenza region, before eventually receiving commissions from the nobility of Venice. His legendary *I Quattro Libri dell' Architettura*, 'The Four Books of Architecture', were published in 1570, laying down his architectural principles, which are still followed by practising architects today.

In the Early and High Renaissance classical revivalism was at its peak, and the Palladian style adhered to classical Roman principles. Drawing inspiration from his studies of the Roman architect Vitruvius, Palladio answered the need for structures that were magnificent but affordable, comfortable but practical, by combining three main elements – dramatic exterior motifs, economical materials and harmonious internal floor plans.

Palladio ultimately developed three primary types of exterior. The simplest consisted of a loggia with three openings. The second was inspired by Greek temple fronts and incorporated – into private residences – a Greek pediment and columns. The third and most modern of the three motifs featured a double-columned loggia, i.e. a complete row of columns on both the ground floor and the floor above.

The Palladian style became fashionable all over Europe. In Britain, Inigo Jones and Christopher Wren embraced it, as did the architect Lord Burlington, who designed Chiswick House in London. To this day, many luxury homes continue to be built according to

Palladio's Villa Rotonda, Vicenza, Italy

Palladio's principles. However, only original villas executed by Palladio himself should be designated 'Palladio villas'; newer structures built according to his principles are built in the 'Palladian style', and are now usually referred to as mansions or similar.

Mediterranean villa

The term 'Mediterranean villa' is usually used to describe a single-family home, influenced by Italian- or Spanish-style architectural detailing. The concept did not actually originate in a Mediterranean country, as is often assumed, but rather in the US. There, it was born as a mixture of two architectural styles – the Spanish Colonial Revival Style and the Mediterranean Revival Style, which eventually became more and more fused.

The Spanish Colonial Revival Style developed in the early twentieth century and was based on the architectural style of the early North and South American Spanish colonies; the Revival updated these forms for a new era. It shared many elements with the Mission Revival and Pueblo styles of the American West and Southwest, and was strongly influenced by the Arts and Crafts Movement, which in turn had informed these latter styles. Spanish Colonial Revival Style is marked by the use of typical Spanish and Mexican materials, often incorporating stucco wall finishes, flat or low-pitched clay-tile roofs, and terracotta or cast-concrete ornaments. Other characteristic elements are small porches or balconies, Roman or semi-circular arcades and fenestration, canvas awnings and decorative iron trim.

The Mediterranean Revival Style, inspired by a resurgence of interest in sixteenth-century Italian Renaissance palaces, first evolved in the US around the turn of the nineteenth century and was popularized in the 1920s and '30s. The style can be found mainly in California and Florida – coastal regions with an affinity to Mediterranean resorts. Mediterranean Revival Style buildings are generally multi-storey and are characterized by stucco wall finishes, arches, and flat or low-pitched terracotta and tile roofs. Other typical features are wrought-iron or wood balconies and window grilles. Many so-called Mediterranean villas also combine elements of other architectural movements, such as Spanish Mission architecture.

Modern/contemporary villa

Another popular style for a luxury home is the 'modern villa'. Of course, a 'modern' or 'modernistic' villa can mean almost anything, just as 'modern architecture' is a very broad term given to a number of building styles with similar characteristics. Generally speaking, however, it describes a style that strives primarily for the simplification of form and the elimination of ornament.

The style first evolved around 1900, and by the 1940s had been consolidated and identified as the 'International Style', eventually becoming the dominant way of building for several decades in the twentieth century. Modern architecture's ambassadors have included, among many others, Adolf Loos, I. M. Pei, Le Corbusier, Louis Kahn, Louis Sullivan, Oscar Niemeyer, Otto Wagner, Philip Johnson and Walter Gropius. But from the point of view of the luxury real-estate market, probably the most influential architects of all are Richard Neutra, Ludwig Mies van der Rohe and Frank Lloyd Wright.

The Austrian Richard Neutra (1892–1970) studied under Adolf Loos and was influenced by Otto Wagner. After moving to the US in the 1920s, he worked briefly for Frank Lloyd Wright before accepting an invitation to live and work communally in Rudolf Schindler's King's Road House in California. Later establishing his own architectural practice in Los Angeles, Neutra was responsible for shaping the California Modern Style that is still influential all around the world. The mid-1990s revival of mid-century modernism has given new cachet to Neutra's work. Along with that of Rudolf Schindler and also John Lautner, it has become trophy property for figures such as designer Tom Ford and actress Kelly Lynch.

Mies van der Rohe (1886–1969), famous for his poetic aphorisms such as 'less is more' and 'God is in the details', made use of modern materials like steel and glass to define his austere but elegant spaces. He is probably best known for his Barcelona Pavilion of 1929 (a reproduction is now built on the original site) and his iconic Villa Tugendhat in Brno, Czech Republic, completed in 1930. His most significant projects in the US – to which he emigrated from Germany in 1937 – include 860–880 Lake Shore Drive, Crown Hall, the Seagram Building and the Farnsworth House.

Mies van der Rohe's Farnsworth House, Illinois, USA

Frank Lloyd Wright's Suntop House, Ardmore, Pennsylvania, USA

that would allow Trent Jones to redesign his original golf-course layout of ten years previously, and would also provide space for the construction of highly exclusive private villas along the course. Ortiz-Patiño renamed the course Valderrama after the ancient estate on which the land was situated; since then, it has risen in golf world rankings to become the No. 1 golf course in mainland Europe, and has hosted such tournaments as the Volvo Masters, the Ryder Cup and the World Golf Championships.

Frank Lloyd Wright (1867–1959) worked in a series of styles over his long career and influenced the whole course of American architecture. To this day, he probably remains America's most famous architect. Having started out with the 'Prairie Houses' of early twentieth-century Chicago, he went on to pioneer some of the most innovative building styles of the period. His most famous private residence is Fallingwater, constructed in Pennsylvania from 1935 to 1939. Among the enormous number of significant projects he left behind is the Solomon R. Guggenheim Museum in New York City, a building that occupied him for sixteen years (1943–1959) and is probably his most recognized masterpiece.

CHALET

A chalet is usually defined as 'a wooden dwelling with a sloping roof and widely overhanging eaves'. The term originally designated such structures in Switzerland and other Alpine regions, but is nowadays used for any lodge built in this style around the globe, be it in Gstaad, Switzerland or Aspen, Colorado.

DEVELOPMENT

The term 'development' usually designates a residential – and often enclosed – community that has been created by a developer from scratch. A developer typically acquires land without any improvements or infrastructure and 'develops' it by establishing utility connections, roads, earth grading, covenants and entitlements. These 'infrastructure improvements' are the basis for 'built improvements', i.e. the construction of dwellings such as villas and other amenities such as golf courses, polo facilities, and so on.

One well-known luxury development is the Valderrama golf development in Sotogrande, Spain. Jaime Ortiz-Patiño, grandson of Bolivia's 'king of tin' Simon Patiño, was one of the first to build a house in Sotogrande. In 1984 he acquired Las Aves, the local golf course designed by Robert Trent Jones, Sr., one of the great golf-course architects. In addition Ortiz-Patiño acquired parcels of land

TYPES OF OWNERSHIP

Property law is a highly developed field of law in almost every country, and it would be overly ambitious to try to describe the various nuances of real-estate legal practice all around the globe. The overview that follows – of the different kinds of property ownership as they tend to occur in most international jurisdictions – is therefore brief, and should be followed up by proper counsel and consultation in whatever market applies.

FULL OWNERSHIP
(FEE SIMPLE, FREEHOLD)

'Full ownership' is used to describe the most complete ownership interest possible in real estate. It usually denotes absolute ownership of real property only limited by government powers (taxation, eminent domain, police power and escheat), certain private or public encumbrances, or conditions in the property title, known as the 'deed'. A full owner not only has the right to own the property during his lifetime, but can also determine its fate after his death (e.g. he can bequeath it via a will to his heirs).

In countries with the common law legal system, such ownership is called 'fee simple' – ownership of an estate in land under common law. This is the usual way real estate is owned in countries that practice common law, such as the US and the UK.

Under English common law theory, the Crown is the ultimate 'owner' of all land but can grant an abstract entity, an estate in land, i.e. the property. The fee simple estate is also called 'estate in fee simple' or 'fee-simple title', and often simply 'freehold' in England and Wales.

JOINT/PARTIAL OWNERSHIP
(CONDOS AND CO-OPS)

Most jurisdictions around the world also have legal mechanisms in place for the part-ownership of real estate, for example for an apartment in an apartment building. Such joint ownership can usually be achieved by using one of two legal constructions, part-ownership of an apartment as a 'condominium' or as a 'cooperative'.

Condos (condominiums)

Real estate owned as a condominium is typically owned in fee simple but subject to rules in the 'declaration of condominium' or created by the 'condominium association'. Such rules may include the payment of monthly fees for maintaining the property's communal areas.

Co-ops (housing cooperatives)

With regard to luxury residential real estate, a housing cooperative (a 'co-op') designates a legal mechanism whereby residents own shares ('share capital co-op') reflecting their equity in the co-operative's real estate. In 'market-rate housing co-ops', members can sell their shares whenever they like, for whatever price the market will bear, much like any other residential property. This type of co-op is very common in New York City.

Prospective owners of an apartment in such a co-op usually have to be approved by the co-op board, a committee of owners of the apartment building. These committees are known to operate on a highly arbitrary basis, and many have rejected even the wealthiest and most illustrious of potential buyers.

TEMPORARY OWNERSHIP
(LEASEHOLD)

Leasehold is a form of property tenure under common law whereby a party buys the right to occupy land or a building for a given length of time. A lease is a legal estate, and leasehold estate can be bought and sold on the open market just like full ownership (i.e. in fee simple) of a property. Until the end of the lease period (often measured in decades, though a 99-year lease is quite common in the UK), the leaseholder has the right to remain in occupation as an assured tenant. Terms of the agreement are contained in a lease that has both contract and property law characteristics.

Such a leasehold differs from a tenancy whereby a property is let on a periodic basis (e.g. weekly or monthly). A lease in rental terms creates a tenancy at will, terminable or renewable at the end of a short period.

The common law of landlord-tenant relations developed in the UK over hundreds of years, and still retains many archaic terms and principles derived from a time when relationships governing the use of land were centred on the promotion of a feudal agrarian society.

FRACTIONAL OWNERSHIP/
CLUB MEMBERSHIP

Two new forms of ownership for luxury residential real estate are currently emerging – so-called 'fractional ownership' and 'club membership'. Both have their roots in the timeshare concept that first appeared in Europe in the mid-1960s. The idea behind timesharing is a form of joint vacation property 'ownership' in which both the use and the costs of running one or several resorts are shared among the multiple owners. In the early 1980s the industry began to show significant signs of expansion, especially in the US, but due to the often mediocre quality of the resorts, the restrictive terms of use, the high prices and difficult re-sale procedures, over time the timeshare concept developed a rather mixed reputation. However, in the wake of the luxury real-estate boom of the late 1990s, it has been taken up and transformed to create an appealing product for a 'money-rich and time-poor' international clientele.

In order to avoid association with the unfortunate timeshare, both the new models – 'fractional ownership' and 'club membership' – are commonly positioned as a clever alternative to outright second-home ownership, offering instead an attractive 'membership' programme. 'Club' is a constant theme, and the 'exclusivity' of the resort environment is usually highlighted. Problems associated with the old timeshare model are circumvented by the much improved property-to-owner/member ratio, plus guaranteed buy-back options.

Fractional ownership

The concept of 'fractional ownership' was first successfully introduced in the US in upscale ski resorts, followed by golf, beach and finally urban destinations. The niche is now growing in other locations around the globe, including the Caribbean, Middle East, South Africa and Europe. Big brands such as Four Seasons, Ritz-Carlton, St Regis and Fairmont are also entering the market. Fractional owners typically take on a deeded ownership that allows them the use of a property within a resort for two to twelve weeks a year, with a very high level of service and amenities. Buyers therefore have access to a luxury residence in a prime destination at a fraction of the cost of an outright second home. They also enjoy a full service model, thus avoiding the burdens usually associated with second-home ownership. Fractional ownership starts at around US$1,000 per square foot, and can often be financed like a traditional real-estate purchase.

Club membership

'Destination clubs' are private clubs that require a one-time 'refundable' membership fee and annual usage dues (similar to those of a country club). Members usually have the right to use multiple luxury residences in different locations within the club. In contrast to the fractional ownership model, club membership does not grant legal ownership of actual real estate, and financing is not commonly available. Club membership is positioned as a leisure lifestyle product, offering similar advantages to fractional ownership, i.e. usage of a luxury residence in a resort destination without the burdens and high costs of traditional second-home ownership. Well-known destination clubs include The Leading Residences of the World, Exclusive Resorts and Private Escapes.

How to Buy … and What to Pay

Although the process of acquiring real estate often appears to be similar in most countries, the actual legal parameters differ quite significantly from country to country. For instance, in France any private contract, even if only oral, can conceivably constitute a binding sales agreement; in Germany, on the other hand, only a notarized sales contract will create binding legal obligations.

In the same vein, the costs associated with the acquisition of real estate not only differ from country to country, but even from city to city within the same country. Thus, buyers in the south may pay a vastly different commission to buyers in the north.

Since both the financial and legal stakes tend to be high when it comes to acquiring luxury property, the overview that follows considers the most significant legal and financial factors in some of the most important luxury markets around the world.

FRANCE

In general, real estate can be acquired by simple agreement. However, the purchase process usually consists of two steps. First, a pre-contract is entered into. One type of pre-contract is the 'promesse de vente', giving the buyer an option to buy within a certain period of time for an agreed price in return for a forfeitable deposit (up to 10% of the sales price). The most common form of pre-contract, however, is the 'compromis de vente', which is a binding sales contract that contains the terms of the sale. This may contain a number of conditions – such as granting of a loan – upon which the validity of the sale is dependent. The second step in the process is signature of the final sales contract, or 'acte authentique', before a notary who is obliged to carry out comprehensive research regarding possible encumbrances prior to the sale. After the notarized sales contract has been entered into, the buyer is registered with the official French property register. Many controls are requested from the seller to protect the buyer. Furthermore, buyers are given seven days after signature of the pre-contract to change their mind without any penalty.

Associated costs may include notary fees (2% to 2.5%) and property purchase tax/registration costs (approximately 4.5% to 5.5%). Real-estate broker commissions vary, but are mostly around 5% of the purchase price. In most cases, the commission will be paid by the seller of the property.

GERMANY

A valid sale of real estate requires a notarized sales contract. The notary will draft the sales agreement and confirm the (non-)existence of possible encumbrances. Payment is subsequently made as stipulated in the notarized sales agreement. Upon completion, the sale is registered with the local land registry, the 'Grundbuch', and ownership is transferred.

Associated costs may include legal fees, notary and registration fees (approximately 2% to 2.3% of the purchase price) and property transfer tax (approximately 3.5%). Real-estate broker commissions vary, but are mostly around 3% to 6% of the purchase price. In most cases, the commission will be paid by the seller of the property. However, commissions may also be split between buyer and seller in some regions.

ITALY

Property ownership can be acquired through a written or notarized contract. Usually the sales process consists of two steps. First, a binding pre-contract, the 'contratto preliminare' or 'compromesso', is entered into, in which the parties agree to enter the final notarized sales contract, or 'rogito', which contains all elements of the final agreement. A deposit (10% to 30% of the purchase price) is usually made at that time. Prior to that, buyers should verify formal ownership, past payment of property taxes and validity of building permits. The pre-contract may be preceded by a 'proposta d'acquisto', or binding formal offer to buy. Ownership of the property is transferred by entering into the 'rogito', or by notarizing an earlier private contract. Subsequently, the sale is registered with different public registers.

Associated costs may include legal fees (approximately 2%), notary fees (approximately 4%) and property purchase taxes (approximately 4% to 10%). Real-estate broker commissions vary, but are mostly around 3% to 5% of the purchase price for sellers. In some cases, a commission of approximately 2% to 3% may also be paid by the buyer of the property.

RUSSIA

In general, the valid purchase of real estate in Russia requires a notarized sales agreement. The notary will draft the agreement and confirm the (non-)existence of possible encumbrances. Payment is subsequently made as stipulated in the notarized sales agreement. Both wire transfers and cash payments are possible payment options. The notarized sales agreement requires registration with the regional State Real Estate Committee. The registration process usually takes between one and two weeks, after which the purchaser is issued a registered property certificate. Deposits usually amount to 10% of the purchase price. When investments in developments under construction are made, an investment contract is signed between investor and developer. Notarization is not required, and registration with the State Real Estate Committee is optional. Payment is made prior to completion of the construction in instalments as stipulated in the contract. The first instalment usually amounts to no less than 30% of the total purchase price. Upon completion of construction, the investor will receive a certificate of registered rights to the property.

Associated costs include notary fees (approximately 1.5%) and annual property tax (0.1% to 0.3%). Commissions (3% to 4%) are paid in most cases by the seller or developer.

SPAIN

In general, property can be acquired by simple agreement, preferably written. However, since registration with the property register requires a notarized sales contract, the sales process usually consists of two steps. First, a binding written sales contract between buyer and seller is entered into containing the terms of the sale. At that time, a deposit of approximately 10% of the purchase price is usually made. Prior to that, buyers should verify ownership with the Land Registry. Other items worth checking are habitation permission, property taxes due and possible existing rental contracts. Secondly, the notarized sales contract, or 'escritura publica', is entered into, which allows the sale to be registered with the Spanish Land Registry. The registration process is usually handled by specialized agencies, known as 'gestorias'.

Associated costs may include property purchase tax or VAT (around 7% tax for existing structures, VAT for newly developed structures). In addition, there are notary and registration fees that are fixed on the basis of a scale. A Spanish particularity is 'plusvalia', a municipal tax on the increase in value on the land. Although it is intended to be paid by the seller, it may be the subject of negotiation between buyer and seller. The 'plusvalia' is to be distinguished from the capital gains tax payable by the seller on profits made when selling the property. Real-estate broker commissions vary, but are mostly around 4% to 6% of the purchase price. In most cases, the commission will be paid by the seller of the property.

SWITZERLAND

Due to recent law changes, citizens of the European Union are now able to acquire real estate without any restrictions if they establish their legal residence in Switzerland. However, the purchase of secondary residences is still subject to numerous restrictions. Financially independent foreigners, such as international entrepreneurs, who establish their legal residence in Switzerland without working there, may take advantage of the possibility of negotiating an individual tax agreement, or 'Pauschalsteuerabkommen', with the tax authorities of the local canton. A tax agreement like this allows individuals to be taxed only on their average cost of living; neither foreign income nor capital is taxed. Real estate is purchased by means of a notarized sales contract. Ownership is transferred with registration with the land registry, or 'Grundbuch'.

Associated costs include notary fees (approximately 0.5% to 1% plus VAT), property purchase tax ('Handänderungssteuer', 1% to 1.5%) and fees for a compulsory property evaluation. Real-estate broker commissions vary, but are mostly between 3% to 6% of the purchase price. In most cases, the commission will be paid by the seller of the property.

UNITED KINGDOM

Prior to the final sales agreement, a formal offer to buy – subject to survey and contracts – will usually be made. A binding agreement to buy is then made through an exchange of private contracts at which the parties will be represented by legal counsel. At that time, a deposit of around 10% of the purchase price is usually placed in an escrow account with the seller's lawyer. Completion is then fifteen to thirty days later. Following the final sale, new ownership is registered with the Land Registry.

Associated costs include stamp duty (between approximately 1% and 4%), legal fees (approximately 1%) and registry fees. Real-estate broker commissions vary, but are mostly around 2% to 3% of the purchase price. The commission will be paid by the seller of the property. Buyers may sometimes be represented at their own expense.

UNITED STATES

In the US, the majority of residential sales contracts are written by licensed real-estate agents using standard forms provided by the National Association of Realtors (NAR) or its local counterparts. These forms were developed by attorneys to comply with local laws and regulations, and are usually a safe way to proceed. However, for more important properties and/or complicated transactions, it is not unusual to have a sales contract drawn up by legal counsel.

Issue of the sales contract is usually preceded by a formal offer from the buyer. Here, too, it is not unusual for home buyers to ask their attorneys to draft offers for them. An offer will often be contingent on a home inspection which gives the buyer certainty about the condition of the house, and can help avoid the purchase of a property that needs major repairs. Inspections are typically paid for by the buyer. Some US states also require sellers to supply a residential property disclosure that describes the condition of all systems in the home.

Other contract contingencies can include specialized inspections (such as for termites, other pests, septic systems and radon levels), appraisal requirements, financing provisions, a description of items sold with the home, or clarification of association dues.

Once the offer is accepted by the seller, the property goes into 'escrow' or 'closing'. The term 'escrow agent' usually describes a title company, attorney or other specialist specifically hired to handle the closing of the sales transaction, including the holding of the buyer's deposit in a neutral escrow account and the preparation of sales documents. In addition to the preparation of the deed, typical steps in the closing process include title searches and the acquisition of title insurance for the buyer.

Closing costs usually amount to approximately 4% of the purchase price, and include such items as title policies, escrow or closing costs, notary fees, attorney's fees, recording and transfer taxes. Real-estate broker commissions are usually between 5% and 6%; if the buyer is represented by his own agent, the fee will usually be split between the buying and the selling agent.

THE MOST IMPORTANT LUXURY MARKETS WORLDWIDE

NEW YORK

New York is without a doubt one of the world's most important luxury markets, currently rivalled only by London. The territory was 'discovered' in the sixteenth century by Giovanni da Verrazzano, an Italian who named it 'New Angoulême' after his patron, King François I of France, who also happened to be the Count of Angoulême. The first colonial settlements were established in the early seventeenth century by the Dutch, who operated a lucrative fur trade with the Native Americans in the region. The Dutch soon baptized the territory 'New Netherland'. When they turned their attention to the island the native Lenape Indians called 'Manna-hatta', they did not simply take the land; eager even then to do the politically correct thing, they 'acquired' it from the Indians as prescribed by Dutch law. One of the leaders of the settlement, Peter Minuit, bought it for 60 guilders' worth of 'trade goods' – an amount equivalent to perhaps US$300 in today's currency. Considering a single square metre of prime Manhattan real estate now costs anywhere between $10,000 and $50,000, this transaction can easily be described as the worst real-estate deal in history....

Having changed the settlement's name to 'New Amsterdam', the Dutch – due to one of those hostilities so frequent in the Old World, this time a war between England and Holland – had to hand the colony over to the English. They, in turn, re-named it 'New York' after the English king's brother, the Duke of York (later King James II). The British left New York in 1783, after American independence was eventually recognized by other countries. The city then briefly (1788–1790) became the capital of the newly founded United States of America.

The early nineteenth century saw the establishment of a geometric street system on the island; the opening of the Erie canal linking New York to the Midwest; and, from 1858 onwards, the creation of Central Park. As one of the major Atlantic ports of entry into the US, a gateway to the rest of the country, and a financial trading centre thanks to the stock exchange founded in 1792, New York quickly became a magnet for immigrants from all over the world, leading to explosive growth. The original Dutch settlement had consisted of some 300 inhabitants; by 1790 there were more than 50,000; and only a hundred years later the city had a population of over 2.5 million.

This growth was, of course, also reflected in the city's real-estate market. Up until the nineteenth century, traditional brownstone houses dominated much of the cityscape. Although these houses came in various architectural styles – Federal, Greek Revival, Gothic Revival and Second Empire, for example – they were all essentially two- to four-storey row houses. In the mid-eighteenth century, however, the first multi-storey apartment buildings began to appear in places such as the Upper West Side, joined by large-scale public

Singer and Woolworth buildings, New York City, early 1900s

buildings like Carnegie Hall. These developments culminated in the appearance of the first skyscrapers in the late nineteenth and early twentieth centuries. Most of the very early examples, such as the 1890 New York World Building, with 20 floors and a height of 105 metres (345 ft), or the 1908 Singer Building with some 47 floors rising over 185 metres (605 ft), have now been demolished. But there are some, such as the Woolworth Building, the Chrysler Building and the Empire State Building, that are still standing and have become landmarks. Today New York – with nearly 200 buildings over 150 metres (490 ft) high – is the city with the highest density of skyscrapers in the world.

From the nineteenth century onwards, the Upper East Side, located from 59th to 96th Street between Central Park and the East River, was one of the most sought-after addresses in Manhattan. Industrialists, including Andrew Carnegie and Henry Clay Frick, built huge mansions opposite the park on Fifth Avenue, which soon became known as 'Millionaire's Row'. Frick's house, designed by the architectural firm of Carrère and Hastings, cost the then-enormous sum of US$5 million; from the start it was designed to accommodate Frick's world-class art collection, which he intended to leave to the public on his death, along with the house, thus imitating what the Marquess of Hertford had done with the Wallace Collection in London some years earlier (the Frick Collection still occupies the Fifth Avenue building to this day). Other financial heavyweights including the Astors, the Rhinelanders and the Schermerhorns built 'country estates' along 86th Street. Indeed, William Backhouse Astor increased his family's real-estate holdings to such an extent that he became known as 'New York's slum landlord'. (His grandson, John Jacob Astor IV, died in the sinking of the Titanic, leaving his son in turn a comfortable inheritance of some $100 million. William Waldorf Astor established the English branch of the family by moving to England in 1890 and becoming a British citizen in 1899; he bought the *Pall Mall Gazette*, etsablished the *Pall Mall Magazine* and funded the Liberal party, eventually acquiring a peerage as baron of

Hever Castle in 1916 and viscount in 1917 – this latter title having reportedly cost him £1 million in donations to prime minister David Lloyd George's slush fund.) Today the Upper East Side – with Fifth Avenue, Madison Avenue and Park Avenue – boasts some of the highest real-estate prices in the world, and features a concentration of wealth found in very few other locations around the globe.

The Upper West Side – extending north from Columbus Circle at 59th Street up to 110th Street, and bordered by Central Park West and Riverside Park – has always been the bohemian sister to the more conservative Upper East Side. Attracting a more intellectual and creative population than its eastern counterpart, the neighbourhood is also home to the oldest Baptist congregation in the US, as well as the oldest Spanish and Portuguese Jewish communities. The Upper West Side houses the New York State Theatre, the New York City Ballet, the New York City Opera, the Metropolitan Opera and the famous Lincoln Center for the Performing Arts. However, although its inhabitants may have been known for their liberal and artistic ways, they have also tended to belong to the moneyed classes, as evidenced in the neighbourhood's elegant, pre-war apartment buildings and beautiful townhouses. Probably the best-known building is the Dakota on 72nd Street and Central Park West (home to John Lennon, who was shot on the steps of its entrance, and also filmed by Roman Polanski for *Rosemary's Baby*, though he was denied permission to film the interior). At the time of its construction (1880–1884), it was in such a remote and isolated position on the Manhattan peninsula that New Yorkers joked it was probably in the territory of the local Native American tribe, the Dakota Indians. The architectural style of the building is often described as castle-like but it is, in fact, more closely related to that of a North German Renaissance town hall. The 65 original apartments featured such amenities as 4-metre-high (13 ft) ceilings, inlaid parquet floors, dumbwaiters, electricity, central heating and tennis courts, making it a huge success among New York society right from the start. Other famous buildings include the San Remo (home to Rita Hayworth, Dustin Hoffman, Paul Simon and Diane Keaton, to name but a few) and The Kenilworth.

Meanwhile, for centuries Downtown New York was regarded as un-chic. This changed with the transformation of SoHo from an industrial neighbourhood to one of the hottest real-estate markets in the US. SoHo (or 'South of Houston [Street]', not to be confused with London's Soho), was originally known as the Cast Iron district due to its many nineteenth-century cast-iron building structures. These mostly housed factories and warehouses, and could be found along the cobblestoned roads of Houston Street, West Broadway, Canal Street and Crosby Street. In the 1960s SoHo was supposed to become the site of two major highways connecting the Manhattan and Williamsburg Bridges on the east with the Holland Tunnel on the west but, thanks to the efforts of the then-fledgling Historical Preservation movement, this plan was soon abandoned, leaving the cast-iron structures intact. Having been abandoned by their original industrial users, they were re-discovered in the 1970s as artists' studios. Young residential tenants then laboriously converted the huge warehouses into lofty, open living spaces, i.e. 'lofts'. What began in the 1970s as an at best semi-legal – if not outright illegal – movement, began during the boom years of the 1980s to attract Young Urban Professionals, aka Yuppies, looking for affordable, yet fashionable new quarters. Galleries, boutiques and restaurants soon followed, turning the once-industrial district into a hip neighbourhood with soaring real-estate prices and tourists en masse, and making it into one of the most sought-after and expensive neighbourhoods of New York City to this day. Such gentrification was not limited to SoHo (or the US for that matter). Other New York neighbourhoods underwent a similar development, including TriBeCa and today's super-trendy Meatpacking District.

LONDON

London is probably the only city in the world that can truly challenge New York's claim to being the world's most important luxury real-estate market.

The capital of the UK has seen its fair share of mixed inhabitants over the past two thousand years. Founded in AD 43, when it was known as Londinium, the city first prospered under the Romans. After they had left in the fifth century, the Anglo-Saxons took over and re-established the city as an important trading centre, changing its name to Lundenvic, Lundenbourgh and Ealdwic. Apart from some Viking raids in the ninth century and a Danish siege in the eleventh century, the Anglo-Saxons controlled the city and the country for almost five hundred years, culminating in the peaceful and prosperous reign of Edward the Confessor. That changed with the arrival of a Frenchman in 1066.

As (still) so often the case amongst European nobility and royalty, great families tend to be related to each other: the family of Duke William II of Normandy was no exception. The mother of Edward the Confessor was also William's aunt, and this was reason enough for William to claim the English throne upon the death of his cousin. Throughout William's reign, and the rest of the Middle Ages, London flourished as a political and economic centre. There were, of course, setbacks in the city's growth. More than 70,000 people died during the Great Plague of 1664–65, and only one year later the Great Fire of London destroyed some 13,000 buildings and large parts of the city. The subsequent rebuilding process was supervised by Sir Christopher Wren, responsible not only for the construction or improvement of some sixty landmark buildings including St Paul's Cathedral and Kensington Palace, but also for London's reconstruction as a whole. This process laid the foundations for the city layout as we know it today. At the same time, many members of the local nobility left their historic quarters and established new residences in the West End; the lower classes moved towards London's East End, where the docklands promised work.

As the British Empire grew, so did London, eventually becoming the world's largest city at the height of Britain's power during the nineteenth and early twentieth centuries. After World War II, however, many Londoners moved to the suburbs, and the demise of the London docks signalled the end of an era. The economic boom of the 1980s saw a huge reversal of fortune for London, which attracted international organizations and entrepreneurial individuals from around the globe. In recent years London's financial heart, the City, has made the capital one of the most expensive real-estate markets in the world. With more than 4,000 workers in its financial sectors earning year-end bonuses of over £1 million, in addition to their non-negligible base salaries, it is little wonder that London house prices have reached record levels.

The most exclusive areas of Central London are undoubtedly Mayfair, Belgravia and Chelsea. Mayfair, located between Hyde Park in the west, Oxford Street in the north, Green Park in the south and Regent Street in the east, has been one of the most fashionable residential districts for the past three hundred years. Originally developed in the seventeenth and eighteenth centuries, it is still in large part the private property of the English Crown and the Grosvenor family headed by the Duke of Westminster (the current incumbent is estimated to be the third richest individual in Great Britain). Although the Grosvenor family dates back to the Middle Ages, it owes its title to Richard Grosvenor, an Oxford graduate and Member of Parliament who represented his native Cheshire and was knighted in 1617 and made baronet in 1621, and can trace back its immense fortune in essence to a clever marriage. In 1677 Sir Thomas Grosvenor, 3rd baronet, had the good sense to marry Miss Mary Davies, heiress to some 120 hectares (300 acres) of land on the outskirts of London. As the city grew, this land quickly became prime real estate, laying the foundation – in every sense of the word – for the family's incredible fortune, both financial and social. Sir Richard Grosvenor, 7th baronet, was created Baron Grosvenor in 1761, and in 1784 under King George III became both Viscount Belgrave and Earl Grosvenor. At the coronation of William IV in 1831 the title Marquess of Westminster was bestowed upon Robert Grosvenor, 2nd Earl Grosvenor. Finally, the title of Duke of Westminster was created by Queen Victoria in 1874 and bestowed upon Richard Grosvenor, 3rd Marquess of Westminster. Today, some five hundred roads, squares and buildings bear the names of titles, people and places associated with the family, including Grosvenor Square and South Audley Street. The Grosvenor Group still owns and controls the property holdings of the family; according to its reports, its real-estate assets under management as of 31 December 2005 totalled £9.1 billion. Other notable Mayfair residents have included British monarchs (Queen Elizabeth II), American presidents (Dwight D. Eisenhower), poets (Robert Browning), novelists (W. Somerset Maugham) and rock idols (Jimi Hendrix).

Belgravia, located to the southwest of Buckingham Palace, is another result of the enterprising Grosvenor family's endeavours. As Mayfair was already fully developed by the time Richard Grosvenor, 2nd Marquess of Westminster, became head of the family, he turned his attention to Belgravia. He commissioned the master builder Thomas Cubitt (who would later be responsible for the east front of

Buckingham Palace, and incidentally turn out to be the great-great-grandfather of Camilla Parker Bowles) to design many elements of the new project. The classic white stucco houses around Eaton Square and Belgrave Square are Cubitt's enduring legacy.

In contrast to Mayfair and Belgravia, Chelsea is anything but a planned development. It originated as a Saxon settlement, whose earliest records date back to Edward the Confessor. Since the Middle Ages, however, it has been a sought-after location by the wealthy, and indeed became known as the 'village of palaces'. In the nineteenth century this 'village' was absorbed by the ever-growing metropolis, and in the early twentieth century developed a reputation for being not only a favourite of the aristocracy, but also of more free-minded individuals such as painters and writers. During the Victorian era, painters including Dante Gabriel Rossetti, J. M. W. Turner, James McNeill Whistler, William Holman Hunt and John Singer Sargent, as well as writers such as George Meredith, Algernon Swinburne, Leigh Hunt and Thomas Carlyle, settled and worked there. This tradition was carried on in the Swinging Sixties and early 1970s when the Beatles and the Rolling Stones lived there, and Vivienne Westwood opened her famous boutique on the King's Road. However, very little remains of these bohemian tendencies; not only are the eastern parts of Chelsea near Sloane Street becoming London's favourite high-end shopping destination, but even the western parts extending to the north, once considered 'poor man's quarters', are now regarded as some of the most desirable residential areas in all of London.

Ile de la Cité, Paris, early 1900s

PARIS

Very few city names evoke as many associations as 'Paris'. Whether it's writers, designers, historians, art lovers or just aficionados of the French way of life, Paris seems to strike a chord in almost everyone.

This feeling is not an invention of modern times. The first settlements in the region date as far back as 4200 BC, when even the pharaohs had not yet begun to think about the blueprints for their first pyramids. The city derives its name from the Parisii tribe, who settled in the area around 250 BC. As elsewhere in Europe, the Romans also left their mark. In 52 BC they conquered the region and began to settle on the left bank of the River Seine and on the Ile de la Cité. The town, re-named Lutetia (and later Lutèce), saw the construction of all those amenities that were so dear to the Romans, such as baths, temples, an amphitheatre and, of course, palaces. However, the decline of the Roman Empire some three hundred years later led to the decline of Lutetia as well, and after a few invasions from its Germanic neighbours, very little was left of the former glory of the city. Foreign invasions, however, were far from over: even the Vikings paid a visit during the siege of Paris in AD 885. After that, the counts of Paris rose to power, eventually becoming kings of France in AD 987. Thereafter Paris continued to develop. It became a university city in 1200, an important trading place, and, of course, unfortunately the locus of many of the political upheavals that made life in those early

times so nerve-racking: the Hundred Years War, the French Wars of Religion, the lavish lifestyles of the French kings after Paris was re-instated as the seat of the royal court in 1594, the French Revolution, and the establishment of the first French republic – Paris saw it all.

The transformation of Paris into the city we know today can be dated and traced back to one man and his vision. On 22 June 1853 Baron Georges-Eugène Haussmann was hired as Emperor Napoleon III's building prefect. His brief was to transform Paris from a medieval city into a modern metropolis. In 1850, with over 1.1 million inhabitants, Paris was already one of Europe's largest cities, but more than a third of the inhabitants lived in ancient, multi-storey row houses whose infrastructures dated back to the Middle Ages and formed an impregnable mass of dwellings, shops and tiny streets. Public services such as water and drainage supplies were notably absent, resulting in waves of cholera that ravaged the city.

The rationale behind the re-structuring of Paris, however, was not only to replace the old and often unsafe and unhygienic city quarters with a more efficient street system, better housing and a more hospitable environment for its inhabitants. Another consideration was to create a city in which anti-royalist rebels could not hide, build barricades and use the old complicated infrastructure for guerrilla warfare, as they had done in the uprisings of 1848. Wide boulevards, open squares and strategically placed train stations were not only pleasant to look at, but also allowed the Imperial army to move more easily and to suppress more efficiently the rebel movement. A final, and by no means negligible, consideration on the Emperor's part was to create a city that would demonstrate his status as a leading European ruler to the rest of the world.

Baron Haussmann did not take his duties lightly. It is estimated that he transformed more than 60% of Paris's then-existing structures. Over 25,000 houses were demolished, and over 40,000 newly built. Entire city quarters were knocked down, and with them much of Paris's medieval heritage. The enormous sum of over 500 million French francs was pumped into the transformation of the city. Haussmann developed plans for the Bois de Boulogne, the enormous park in the southwest of Paris, and redesigned the Luxembourg gardens to make way for new streets. He also replaced the former warren of tiny, narrow streets with a new, comprehensive system of wide, tree-lined boulevards. A new water supply, a gigantic sewer system, new bridges, elegant public buildings including the opera house, theatres and market halls (Les Halles) transformed and re-defined the city. A uniform building height and re-organization of the street system, with wide axes and central focal points like the Place de l'Etoile, are only some of the enduring legacies of Haussmann's schemes. Another is the Neo-classical building style used for the reconstruction which today makes Paris one of the world's most elegant cities.

Paris's most sought-after neighbourhoods also date back to the time of this re-organization. The 1st district (1er arrondissement), on the right bank, close to the Louvre and the Place Vendôme (where the legendary Ritz Hotel is located), has always been one of the most desirable addresses in Paris. The same goes for its immediate neighbour, the 8th district (8ème arrondissement): this extremely elegant quarter, which includes Paris's most famous streets, like the Champs-Elysées and the Rue du Faubourg-Saint-Honoré with its presidential palace and the – almost equally famous – Hermès fashion house, is where most of the French, and international, elite lay their head each night, be it in spacious apartments or in so-called hôtels particuliers. These hôtels have nothing to do with hotels, but are, in fact, single-family dwellings much closer in character to 'palais' than to simple 'townhouses'. The façade of an hôtel particulier may not hint at its extraordinary interior, but these hidden gems usually offer huge proportions, sumptuous materials and stately architectural features such as entrance halls with grand staircases, 4-metre-high (13 ft) ceilings, parquet floors, floor-to-ceiling windows, wood-burning fireplaces in most rooms, double doors and fine wood panelling.

The slightly more relaxed and free-minded, bohemian alternative is the 6th quarter (6ème arrondissement), on the left bank of Paris. This quarter is the traditional home of the city's fabled art and antiques dealers as well as the local and international intellectual elite. Many famous artists and writers like Ernest Hemingway, Jean-Paul Sartre and Simone de Beauvoir made their base on the Boulevard Saint-Germain and other nearby streets.

The neighbouring 7th district (7ème arrondissement), with the Eiffel tower, the Champs de Mars park and the Place des Invalides, is the traditional home of Paris's bourgeoisie, just like its counterpart on the right bank, the 16th district (16ème arrondissement).

LOS ANGELES

Los Angeles, or LA as it is most commonly known, is one of the world's most fabled luxury real-estate markets. The largest city in the state of California, and the second most populous city in the US, LA still attracts thousands of people from all over the world hoping to make their fortune there.

The first European visitor was explorer Juan Cabrillo, who in 1542 stopped at what we know today as San Pedro, and was greeted by natives from the Tongvan tribe who had lived in the region for thousands of years. This first visit was to be short-lived, as Cabrillo died later that year; no European was seen again for almost 250 years. It was on 4 September 1781 that 44 Spanish settlers gathered at San Gabriel Mission and gave a small town in the vicinity the catchy name of 'El Pueblo de Nuestra Señora Reina de los Ángeles sobre El Rio Porciuncula', or 'The Town of Our Lady Queen of the Angels on the Porciuncula River' – or simply 'Los Angeles'. After belonging to Spain for the next forty years, the town subsequently became part of Mexico when Mexico gained independence from Spain in 1821. However, California again changed hands in 1848 when Mexico had to cede it to the United States at the conclusion of the Mexican-American War.

On 4 April 1850 Los Angeles was incorporated as a city. In fact in the 1870s it was still little more than a village, with a population of just 5,000. Only fifty years later, however, there were already over 100,000 inhabitants. Several factors were responsible for the sudden growth. One was that oil was discovered by Edward L. Doheny in 1892, making Los Angeles a centre of oil production in the early twentieth century, producing a mere 25 years later one-quarter of the world's total supply.

Another factor was a canny development scheme devised by a close-knit group of people determined to expand the city and make a fortune in the process. From 1899 onwards, Harrison Gray Oris and his son-in-law Harry Chandler began buying up cheap land in the San Fernando Valley on the northern outskirts of Los Angeles. At the same time they enlisted the help of William Mulholland, then chief engineer of the Los Angeles Water Department, and J. B. Lippencott, employee of the United States Reclamation Service. Lippencott performed water surveys in the Owens Valley and managed to persuade Owens Valley farmers and mutual water companies to pool their interests and surrender the water rights to some 80,000 hectares (200,000 acres) of land to his agent. Lippencott then resigned from the Reclamation Service and took a job as an assistant to Mulholland in the Los Angeles Water Department, bringing with him as a welcome gift the Reclamation Service maps, field surveys and stream measurements. These studies would serve as the basis for the design of the longest aqueduct in the world. Now the next phase in the grand scheme was about to be revealed. By July 1905, Chandler's influential newspaper, the *Los Angeles Times*, had begun to warn the people of Los Angeles that the county would be faced with serious drought problems unless they voted bonds for building the aqueduct. Simultaneously, an artificial drought was created by running water into the sewers in order to deplete the reservoirs; residents were also forbidden to water their gardens. Unsurprisingly, on election day the people of Los Angeles voted for $22.5 million worth of bonds to build an aqueduct from the Owens River. Using this money, and backed up by a special Act of Congress allowing cities to own property outside their boundaries, the City of Los Angeles acquired the land that Lippencott's agent had bought from the Owens Valley farmers and started to build the aqueduct. Mullholland's memorable speech on the occasion of the grand opening on 5 November 1913 consisted of five words: 'There it is. Take it.'

Also fostering Los Angeles's growth was the then-burgeoning film industry, as well as the incorporation into the city of communities such as Wilmington (1909), Hollywood (1910) and Venice (1925). These factors, together with the hosting of the 1932 Summer Olympics and the building of the freeways in the 1940s, meant that the city continued to flourish.

The 'Golden Triangle' of Los Angeles's most expensive and exclusive neighbourhoods is comprised of Beverly Hills, Bel Air and Holmby Hills. Beverly Hills started out as a dry oil well of the Amalgamated Oil Company. In 1906 the property passed into the hands of a new development firm, the Rodeo Land and Water Company, who designed a new town with large lots for homes and broad, curving streets lined with a wide variety of trees. The inspiration for the name of this new town came when the company's president happened to read a newspaper article that mentioned Beverly Farms, Massachusetts; he suggested the name 'Beverly Hills' for the project, and, after a shaky start during the economically unstable years of 1907 and 1908, in 1910 the first houses went up. A boom-time followed when

Bugsy Siegel's 35-room mansion, Beverly Hills, Los Angeles

The Beverly Hills Hotel was built in 1912 and immediately became the centre of social life in the area: everything was conducted in the hotel, from marriages and Sunday church services to grand balls and screenings in the only motion picture theatre. The first movie stars to settle in Beverly Hills were Douglas Fairbanks and Mary Pickford, who bought land on Summit Drive in 1919 and built a house which they aptly named 'Pickfair'. Other wealthy members of the movie community soon followed. In 1928 Harold Lloyd built his mansion in Benedict Canyon, followed by John Barrymore, Robert Montgomery and Miriam Hopkins, thereby establishing Beverly Hills's reputation for being the home of choice for the rich and famous – a reputation that still continues.

Bel Air, on the west side of the city, was the brain-child of a certain Alphonzo E. Bell, Sr., an oil millionaire, champion tennis player and real-estate developer. Bell's large oil profits had enabled him to invest heavily in large, upscale, real-estate communities in West Los Angeles, including parts of Westwood, Beverly Hills and Pacific Palisades. His masterpiece, however, was the Bel Air Estates, founded in 1922 on more than 240 hectares (600 acres), as an exclusive neighbourhood complete with lush vegetation, new roads, utilities and a world-class country club. Since the 1920s, Bel Air has become one of the most exclusive neighbourhoods in the LA region. One of its many notable residents was former US President Ronald Reagan, who lived at 668 St Cloud Road from his retirement until his death (it is said that the Reagan residence actually used to be 666 St Cloud, but the number was changed as former First Lady Nancy objected to the 'Satanic overtones').

Holmby Hills, in western Los Angeles, is bordered by Beverly Hills to the east and Bel Air to the northwest. The development of Holmby Hills began when Arthur Letts, Sr., the English-born millionaire founder of the Broadway Department Store empire, purchased 160 hectares (400 acres) of a ranch that occupied the terrain. Letts had a vision for the prime acreage he had purchased, at $100 an acre, and that was to create a neighbourhood of impressive estates on large lots. He christened the development 'Holmby Hills' after his birthplace, a small hamlet in England named Holdenby. When Letts died suddenly in 1923 before he could realize his vision, his son-in-law Harold Janss took over the project and soon advertised it as 'The Ultimate in Residential Estate Development'. Luxurious touches included custom-made, English-style street lamps as well as electricity and telephone lines buried underneath the wide, tree-lined streets to preserve the landscape (Letts himself had been an extremely skilled horticulturalist). Thanks to the lush landscaping, enormous lot sizes and ensuing privacy, Holmby Hills attracted the rich and famous from the very beginning. Among the first mansions built in the late 1920s was the Tudor-style home of the founder's son, Arthur Letts, Jr. (the same house would later be purchased by Hugh Hefner and become Playboy Mansion West). Many other celebrities, including Gary Cooper, Barbra Streisand, Aaron Spelling, and Sonny and Cher, have also called Holmby Hills home.

HONG KONG

Hong Kong, the gateway to the Far East, has been an almost mythical place for hundreds of years. Stories about its wealth, powerhouse atmosphere and reputation as a place of opportunity have long attracted people from around the globe.

In fact, Hong Kong is not a mere city, but a collection of over 260 islands in the South China Sea, consisting primarily of Hong Kong Island, Lantau Island, the Kowloon Peninsula and the New Territories that connect the North with mainland China across the Sham Chun River. The name 'Hong Kong', meaning 'fragrant harbour', is derived from the present-day Aberdeen quarters on Hong Kong Island, where fragrant wood products and incense were once traded.

The region became part of Imperial China during the Qin Dynasty around 200 BC, and remained a part of China until the nineteenth century under the Qing Dynasty. Although Hong Kong did have some foreign visitors during these two thousand years (notably an invasion of Mongols in 1276, which prompted the defeated Chinese child emperor to drown himself together with his local court officials), its ascent to an international turning point began through its association with Great Britain. The foundation for Hong Kong's close ties with the British Empire were laid when the legendary East India Company, founded by Royal Charter in 1600 and largely responsible for Britain's incredible overseas expansion over the next three hundred years, established a trading post in nearby Canton.

The fact that Hong Kong eventually became a British colony can, however, really be traced back to the British fondness for tea. By 1830 the British were consuming the astonishing quantity of 30 million pounds of Chinese tea per annum, or an average of 2 pounds per person. Needless to say, the import of such massive quantities was reflected in Britain's trade balance with China: while Britain exported items such as watches and silver to China, this could never make up for the huge trade deficit caused by the Chinese tea imports to Britain. Britain saw a chance to reduce that deficit somewhat by

The Governor's Residence on The Peak, Victoria, Hong Kong, c. 1931

(indirectly) importing into China opium, consumption of which had exploded over the previous century. Chinese objections to opium-trading led to the writing of an official letter to Queen Victoria, asking her to put a halt to the practice. When the Queen did not react, the Chinese commissioner confiscated some 20,000 chests of opium that had found their way into China and burned them. Queen Victoria sent expeditionary forces to defend Britain's 'ancient rights of commerce', thus starting the First Opium War. After a series of Chinese defeats, Hong Kong Island was occupied by British forces in 1841, before being formally ceded to Britain at the end of the war. Victoria City was founded a year later, and Britain established Hong Kong as a Crown Colony. In 1860, following China's defeat in the Second Opium War, Stonecutter's Island and the Kowloon Peninsula south of Boundary Street were also ceded to Britain. Finally, in 1898, Britain obtained a 99-year lease of the adjacent northern lands and Lantau Island, which became known as 'the New Territories'.

British influence drastically altered Hong Kong's character. After the British takeover, Hong Kong was soon declared a free port, enabling traders to import and export goods without having to pay custom duties, thus making Hong Kong a trading hub for the entire region. Merchants, opium traders and merchant bankers from all over the world were drawn to the island (European businessmen were locally referred to as 'tai-pans', quite literally 'big shots'), followed by thousands of Chinese from mainland China hoping to find both work and political refuge in the Crown Colony. As a consequence, the population exploded, laying the foundation for Hong Kong's unparalleled growth over the next hundred years.

When the British first took control in 1841, Hong Kong contained just over 7,500 inhabitants, mostly fishermen. Less than 25 years later, this number had risen to over 125,000. British amenities soon spread, including libraries, post offices, museums, hotels and restaurants, as well as cricket pitches, polo grounds and private members' clubs like the famous Hong Kong Club, founded in 1846. The east of Hong Kong was dominated by the British rulers and their institutions, its west by the native Chinese. To escape Hong Kong's humid, hot summers, the first Europeans began in 1868 to build their summer residences on Victoria Peak, a mountain of some 500 metres (1,640 ft) altitude in the southwestern part of Hong Kong Island. Local residents were at first carried by their staff up the hill in sedan chairs, but from 1888 onwards could rely on a more civilized means of transport – a tram railway. The exclusive character of 'The Peak', as the quarter would become known, was further underlined by official ordinances that permitted only Europeans and government officials to take up residence there. To this day, the Peak remains one of Hong Kong's most exclusive quarters.

By World War I, there were some 725,000 inhabitants in Hong Kong; by World War II more than 1.5 million. Of course, such an active outpost in this part of the world also attracted the attention of the Japanese. On 8 December 1941, during World War II, Imperial Japan invaded Hong Kong, and its British and Canadian defenders were forced to surrender on Christmas Day. During the Japanese occupation, the population of Hong Kong suffered from food shortages and hyper-inflation, and subsequently declined by almost 75% from 1.6 million to approximately 600,000 in 1945, when the United Kingdom resumed control of the colony following Japan's defeat.

Hong Kong's population recovered quickly as refugees from the ongoing Chinese civil war arrived in droves. The proclamation of the People's Republic of China in 1949 only intensified this process; at the same time, more and more corporations from Shanghai and Guangzhou also shifted their operations to Hong Kong, as the Communist government increasingly isolated the country from outside influence, making Hong Kong the only place of contact between mainland China and the rest of the Western world.

Textile and manufacturing industries grew rapidly due to the combination of quick population growth and low manual labour costs. Hong Kong's rapidly industrialized economy became driven by exports to international markets, and living standards rose steadily with the industrial growth. When Communist China initiated its first economic reforms in 1978, Hong Kong became the main source of foreign investments to the mainland; a Special Economic Zone was established the following year in the Chinese city of Shenzhen, located immediately north of the mainland's border with Hong Kong. The economy of Hong Kong gradually shifted from textiles and manufacturing to the services, financial and banking sectors. During the 1970s, Hong Kong developed into the international powerhouse we know today, and a lot of its high-rises date back to that period.

Since the 99-year lease of the New Territories came with an expiry date, the British and Chinese governments met in the 1980s to discuss Hong Kong's sovereignty. In 1984 the two countries signed the Sino-British Joint Declaration, agreeing to transfer sovereignty of Hong Kong to the People's Republic of China in 1997. Even though Hong Kong is thus now officially Chinese again, it continues to be one of the world's most thriving international centres. As China gradually opens up its markets to the West and incredible new wealth is created in what is the world's most populous country, Hong Kong will play a major role as a hub between the Far East and the West.

To this day, the Peak remains the most sought-after real-estate market in Hong Kong. Other highly desirable neighbourhoods include the South Side of Hong Kong Island. However, wherever there is a square metre to spare, real estate will be built. On either side of Victoria Harbour, a forest of skyscrapers has sprung up. Indeed, parts of the old harbour itself have been turned into land that can be built on, and have quickly become the site of major developments.

BERLIN

Berlin's real-estate market is still a 'secret tip' among international investors. How is it that the capital of Germany – indeed, Germany's largest city, with a population of 3.4 million – can still be a 'secret tip'? The answer lies in the city's colourful history.

The earliest records date back to the late twelfth and early thirteenth centuries, but it was in 1415 that the city first became more than just a dot on the map. It was then that the noble family of Hohenzollern under Frederick I was given the Margraviate of Brandenburg, and in 1451 Berlin became the official royal residence of the Brandenburg electors under Frederick II. At this early stage Brandenburg was not much more than swampland and Berlin no more than a provincial town, but the Hohenzollern family were keen to develop their new territory and steadily expanded their realm. After 150 years of growth, however, the Thirty Years' War (1618–1648) intervened and devastated Germany. Berlin lost half its population, and a third of all housing structures were destroyed or damaged.

Fortunately, a new era of prosperity and growth was ushered in under Elector Frederick William, who would subsequently become known as the 'Great Elector'. He initiated a policy of religious tolerance, giving asylum to the French Huguenots with the Edict of Potsdam in 1685. More than 15,000 Huguenots immigrated to Brandenburg, over a third of them settling in Berlin. Thus, by 1700, approximately 20% of Berlin's residents were French, and their cultural influence on the city was immense.

The growth of Berlin and Brandenburg continued under Frederick, who in 1701 had crowned himself 'King of Prussia'. Frederick spared no effort in transforming Berlin into a capital that he deemed worthy of the new 'Kingdom of Prussia', and the city thus became one of the most glittering centres of Europe – to such an extent that English diplomats complained to their London superiors that their meagre funds did not allow them to keep up with the glitz of the Prussian court.

Frederick I of Prussia's successor, in contrast to his predecessor (as is so often the case), was known as the 'Soldier King'. He transformed Prussia into a lean, highly organized state, with serious political and military muscle. But it was, in turn, his son who was to become Prussia's most influential ruler. Ascending to the throne in 1740, Frederick II turned Berlin into the centre of the Enlightenment movement – Europe's capital of art, literature and music – and he himself became known as 'Frederick the Great'.

Following France's victory in the War of the Fourth Coalition, Napoleon Bonaparte marched into Berlin in 1806, but he granted self-government to the city. During the nineteenth century the Industrial Revolution transformed Berlin further; its economy and population expanded dramatically, and it became the main rail hub and economic centre of Germany. Additional suburbs soon developed and increased both the area and population of Berlin. In 1861 outlying suburbs, including Wedding and Moabit, were incorporated into the city. In 1871 Berlin became the capital of the newly founded German Empire.

In 1918, at the end of World War I, the Weimar Republic was proclaimed in Berlin. In 1920 the Greater Berlin Act united dozens of suburban cities, villages and estates into one greatly expanded city, and established Berlin as a separate administrative region. After this expansion, Berlin had a population of around 4 million. In the 1920s

Typical luxury villa, dating from 1890, Berlin

it was one of the world's most exciting cities, known for its liberal subcultures, but also notorious for its increasingly fierce political street fights.

When in 1933 Adolf Hitler and the Nazi Party came to power, Berlin's – and Germany's – darkest chapter began. Many members of the country's intellectual elite fled, and Berlin's flourishing Jewish community, which numbered 170,000 before Nazi rule, was cruelly decimated. During the 1943–45 air raids and the Battle of Berlin, large parts of the city were destroyed. After the war ended, what was once one of Europe's most lively and elegant metropolises had become a gigantic wasteland. Since so many German men had either died in the war or were still prisoners, it was up to the local women to re-build the city. These legendary 'rubble women' ('Trümmer-frauen') literally re-built Berlin stone by stone, salvaging and re-using the old building materials.

After the Treaties of Yalta and Potsdam, the victorious powers divided the city into four sectors, analogous to the occupation zones into which Germany was divided. The sectors of the Western Allies (the US, Britain and France) formed West Berlin, while the Soviet sector formed East Berlin. In theory, all four allies retained shared responsibility for the city. However, political tensions between the Western Allies and the Soviet Union quickly surfaced, prompting the Soviet Union eventually to impose the Berlin Blockade, an economic blockade of West Berlin, by closing the Soviet-controlled territory around the city and thus cutting it off from Western supplies. The allies successfully overcame this by airlifting food and other supplies into Berlin (the famous 'air-bridge' or 'Luftbrücke').

In 1949, the Federal Republic of Germany was founded in West Germany, while the Marxist-Leninist German Democratic Republic (GDR) was proclaimed in East Germany. The founding of the two German states increased Cold War tensions. West Berlin was sur-rounded by East German territory. East Germany, however, proclaimed East Berlin (which it described only as 'Berlin') as its capital, a move that was not recognized by the Western powers. The

tensions between East and West, and the constant stream of inhabi-tants of the Eastern sectors to the Western ones, eventually culminated in the construction of the Berlin Wall by East German authorities on 13 August 1961. From one day to the next, this wall literally cut Berlin in two, dividing thoroughfares, squares and even houses, and separating families living in different sectors. East Berliners made desperate attempts to cross the wall and hundreds lost their lives or were injured trying to get to the other side.

While it was possible for Westerners to pass from one part of Berlin (and Germany) to the other, through strictly controlled check-points, such travel was impossible for Easterners. The two Berlins developed in completely different directions. East Berlin became a showplace for the Socialist GDR, and many important historic build-ings, like the Prussian Royal Palace, were demolished in order to extinguish the Prussian heritage that was deemed 'capitalist', or were utilized as cheap housing and administrative offices, or else were simply left to fall into ruin. At the same time, pre-fabricated housing structures were erected all over the city and heralded as a great Socialist achievement. West Berlin, on the other hand, developed into an 'island of capitalism' in a 'sea of socialism', becoming a highly diverse Western city that drew free-thinkers, artists and international visitors alike.

As a consequence of the Glasnost policy initiated in the 1980s under Russian premier Mikhail Gorbachev, combined with frustra-tion at the old Socialist regime and the growing economic inequality between East and West, the East German liberation movement organized huge political demonstrations. In an attempt to appease the public, on 9 November 1989 a state official declared that freedom of travel would be reinstated 'in some form' – and thus the East German wall was opened more or less by mistake. When demon-strators demanded that the border patrol open the wall, they did so, assuming they were under orders, which was not in fact the case. Tens of thousands of East Berliners streamed into West Berlin, many of them meeting for the first time the families from whom they had been separated for more than thirty years. This led to the official reunification of East and West Germany in 1990, Berlin becoming, once again, the capital of unified Germany.

Over the following years, billions and billions of Euros were invested in updating East Germany and East Berlin to modern Western standards. In anticipation of an economic boom, Germany and Berlin embarked on an incredible building boom: entire quarters were either completely restored or re-built from scratch. The economic upswing, however, has unfortunately failed to materialize thus far, resulting in large over-supplies in housing stock. This slump offers huge potential for long-term investors, as prices for prime real estate currently tend to be among the lowest in any Western European capital.

Traditionally, the most sought-after quarters have been Dahlem, Lichterfelde-West and Wannsee. Dahlem's roots go back to the thir-teenth century, when it used to be the property of the local squire. For more than four hundred years, it remained the private property of noble notables such as the von Spiel, von Pfuhl and von Wilmerstorff families, before it was eventually sold to the Prussian state in 1838. In 1901, it was subdivided to be re-organized as a suburb for the privileged, following an English example (the intention was to create 'a German Oxford'). Since then, it has been one of the most desirable quarters in the Berlin region, with a large number of generously sized villas, mansions and parks.

By contrast, Lichterfelde-West was one of the first entirely planned luxury residential developments in the German Empire. The Hamburg entrepreneur Johann Anton Wilhelm Carstenn, after travelling through England, was inspired to build residential buildings in a green, natural environment. Unlike in England, however, where country houses were, indeed, only to be found in the country, far from a town and usually with little local infrastructure, Carstenn envisioned 'luxury villages' adjacent to big cities, offering large country-style houses with access to a fully developed infrastructure.

After successfully experimenting with a 'luxury colony' in his hometown of Hamburg, Carstenn in 1860 acquired the estates of Lichterfelde and Giesendorf, outside Berlin. He soon began to create local infrastructure by establishing roads and railway connections, though he decided not to build the houses himself but rather to create and sell generous parcels of land, and leave the actual building process to the owners. Within the first few years, he had quickly sold many parcels that way. However, things then turned difficult. In the face of widespread economic crises – the so-called 'Gründer-Crash' – Carstenn decided to give 20 hectares (50 acres) of Lichterfelde-West land to the Prussian state for the erection of a new officer-training academy, reasoning that this would be an incentive for many Prussian officers and their families to move to the region. His strategy proved fruitful: over the next few decades, Lichterfelde-West developed into the town of choice for many noble Prussian families, whose members traditionally served in the army. However, despite the overall success of the development, Carstenn was driven to financial ruin by the obligations he had created with the establishment of the academy and, after receiving ennoblement and the title 'von Carstenn-Lichterfeld', in addition to a modest life pension, from the German emperor Wilhelm I, he died in 1896 in a mental hospital in nearby Schöneberg. Lichterfelde-West, which became part of Berlin in the 1920s, maintained its popularity and has stood the test of time remarkably well, looking today not much different to how it looked 120 years ago. Large town- and country-houses with spacious gardens in a variety of historic architectural styles, ranging from art nouveau to Neo-classical to Neo-gothic, still give this part of town its outstanding character. Many roads still boast their original cobblestone paving, and almost all of them are lined with the majestic trees that were planted over a century ago.

A similar undertaking was the 'Alsen colony', a planned development of highly impressive summer residences around Berlin's biggest lake, the Wannsee. These properties were sold to Berlin's moneyed classes from the 1870s onwards. Like Lichterfelde-West, this district was later incorporated into the city of Berlin, and is nowadays one of its most sought-after residential areas.

THE FRENCH RIVIERA

The French Riviera, or the 'Côte d'Azur' as it is locally known (the term goes back to 1887, when Stephen Liégeard, a French civil servant with literary ambitions, published a book of that name about the coast), is one of the world's most famous seaside resorts. The 'Côte' is usually understood to describe the French Mediterranean coast, stretching from Menton and Monaco near the Italian border all the way through Nice, Antibes and Cannes to St Tropez. There is, however, a never-ending dispute between the local communities as to which of them are actually worthy members of this illustrious club. Many inhabitants of Cannes, for example, would argue that the 'true' Côte d'Azur ends after Théoule-Sur-Mer to the west of the town, whereas the inhabitants of the coast between Cannes and St Tropez would, of course, insist that their homes are on the Côte.

The history of the region dates back to the early history of mankind: Europe's oldest prehistoric site, the Grotto of Le Vallonet at Roquebrune near Monaco, is an impressive million years old, and more than 400,000 years ago, prehistoric man occupied the site today known as Terra Amata. Around the fourth century BC, both the Greeks and the Ligurians settled in the region but, as elsewhere in Europe, it was not long before the Romans arrived. In 154 BC they took over the settlements of Antipolis (Antibes) and Nikaia (Nice) from the Greeks. When the Roman Empire declined, the Côte d'Azur faced a change of ownership. In AD 508 Provence fell into the hands of the Germanic tribes of the East Goths, before the Franks took over in AD 536. The Frankish realm would eventually see the height of its power under Charlemagne and develop into the Holy Roman Empire and France in the ninth century. However, while these nations would flourish, the coast was for most of the ninth and tenth centuries subject to attacks and invasions from the Saracens, before Count William of Provence could eventually fight them off permanently.

During the Middle Ages, the Côte – and especially Nice as its most important centre – saw its fair share of battles, famines and other disasters. The Counts of Provence, the House of Aragon (from Spain),

View of the old town of Cannes, French Riviera, c. 1890

the House of Anjou (from France), the Counts of Savoy (from Italy), the Kingdom of France, as well as the Kingdom of Piedmont-Sardinia, all left their mark in an ongoing stream of changing political alliances, wars and invasions. France eventually acquired the 'Comté de Nice' from Italian Piedmont-Sardinia on 24 March 1860 – a move that had to be confirmed by a public referendum. A new French department was subsequently created, the 'Alpes-Maritimes', which also included Grasse and the surrounding area which had previously been part of the department of Var. This momentous return to 'natural frontiers' was marked by a celebratory visit of Napoleon III and Empress Eugénie to Nice in the autumn of 1860.

The history of the French Riviera as Europe's favourite seaside resort began in the eighteenth century, when members of the English nobility discovered that the mild winter climate and charming landscape offered a tempting alternative to harsh English winters (not to mention summers). In 1901 Queen Victoria reportedly said on her deathbed, 'Oh, if only I were in Nice, I should recover.' It was she who more or less confirmed the Riviera's status when she first visited Menton in 1882. She came to the Riviera on nine subsequent occasions and spent more time there than in any other part of Europe, let alone other parts of her Empire (she famously did not even once visit her biggest possession, India). And, of course, where the 'Grandmother of Europe' and reigning monarch of the then-most powerful nation on earth led, others were sure to follow. Queen Victoria's son, Prince Leopold, Duke of Albany, joined her, hoping to recover in Menton from his ongoing health problems. The Rothschilds followed a few years later, and eventually Royal Highnesses from all over Europe, including Leopold II, the notorious King of the Belgians, became frequent visitors to the Riviera.

In the 1920s, the Côte finally developed from a winter to a summer destination. Two of the first international visitors to stay there in summer were wealthy American expats Gerald and Sara Murphy, who, in turn, attracted a whole host of friends and acquaintances, from Picasso to F. Scott Fitzgerald. How the Murphys persuaded a local hotel owner to keep his hotel open during the summer season is recorded in Fitzgerald's *Tender is the Night* (1934), whose main characters are based on the couple.

The main focal points of the Côte d'Azur were and are Nice (and Cap Ferrat), Cannes (and Cap d'Antibes), Monaco and St Tropez. Among the first of the English to 'discover' Nice were Lord and Lady Cavendish, who visited the city in 1731. Lady Cavendish was heavily pregnant when she arrived and shortly thereafter gave birth to a son, Henry Cavendish (he would later find fame as the chemist who discovered the chemical constitutions of water and atmospheric air). Then, in the wake of the success of the travel book *du jour*, Tobias Smollett's *Travels Through France and Italy*, published in 1766, several members of the British aristocracy followed the Cavendishes to the Côte, among them the Duke of York, the Duke of Gloucester, the Duke of Bedford and the Duchess of Cumberland. Many of the British settled in the Croix de Marbre quarter of Nice, which soon became known as 'Little London'. However, when Napoleon emerged in 1792, the British colonization of Nice came to an abrupt halt, and this only started to resume after Napoleon's defeat at Waterloo in 1815. Gradually the British began to come back and by 1829 there were already up to a hundred British families wintering in Nice.

The establishment of Cannes as a chic resort owes much, if not everything, to the combination of two rather disparate factors: cholera and an English lord. Lord Brougham, a former Lord Chancellor of England, was on his way to Nice in 1834 with his sickly daughter when he was stopped at the Sardinian frontier due to an outbreak of cholera in the region. Forced to retreat, he chose the little fishing village of Cannes as his temporary home. Cannes seems to have played its charms right, as Lord Brougham became so enchanted with the place that he bought a piece of land and built a villa on it. Brougham – a lawyer and a radical (and the inventor of the first four-wheeled carriage intended to be drawn by only one horse) – subsequently left 'Fog-land', as he called England, each winter for the Riviera. He seemed to have had little difficulty in encouraging his friends to follow his example and build there as well, thus laying the foundation for the large British colony in Cannes.

What Lord Cavendish had been for Nice and Lord Brougham for Cannes, Aristotle Onassis was for the principality of Monaco. Born in 1906 a member of the poor Greek minority in Smyrna, Turkey, Onassis and his family had to flee for Greece during the Turkish civil war. He then emigrated at the tender age of 16 to Argentina and laid there the basis for his fortune by selling Turkish tobacco. He used the proceeds from this activity to acquire several old tankers, and business boomed when the tankers exclusively carried Allied war material across the ocean during World War II. After the war, Onassis began building the first supertankers, eventually becoming the worldwide 'tanker king'. Although an ill-fated deal with Saudi Arabia brought him close to ruin, the Suez crisis of 1957 produced a worldwide need for transport capacities and helped him grow his fortune to the then-almost unimaginable sum of US$1 billion. Onassis diversified his holdings subsequently, and invested heavily in other fields of business, among them real estate. In 1954 he fell in love with the principality of Monaco which, at that time, was in rather desolate shape.

Monaco had been ruled by the Grimaldi family – originally from Genoa in Italy – since 1297, when a certain François Grimaldi had disguised himself as a monk and seized the 'Rock of Monaco', a colony of nearby Genoa. Since that time, the Grimaldi family has been ruling the tiny micro-state with its 200 hectares (495 acres) of land as a constitutional monarchy. By the middle of the nineteenth century it had developed into a renowned seaside resort with its own casino, but in the 1950s it was beginning to crumble. International gamblers and pleasure-seekers were a rare sight in the aftermath of World War II, and Monaco's infrastructure began to deteriorate due to lack of maintenance.

The new reigning Prince Rainier III had acceded to the throne under most unusual circumstances. In 1918, it became foreseeable that Prince Louis, the son of the reigning monarch Prince Albert I, would leave no direct, legitimate heir apparent. However, his closest relative, and thus theoretically next in line for the throne, would have been his German cousin, the Duke of Urach. Needless to say, a German duke on the throne of Monaco was unimaginable for France after World War I. As a result, drastic measures were taken. While stationed as an army officer in Algeria, Prince Louis had met the cabaret singer Marie Juliette Louvet with whom he had had an illegitimate child, Charlotte. To prevent Monaco falling into the hands of a German duke, it was decided that Charlotte Louvet should be adopted by Prince Louis. Thus the child became Princess Charlotte Louise Juliette de Grimaldi, Duchess of Valentinois. A special law had to be passed in 1918 to allow such an adoption with the ensuing transfer of title and rights. When Louis II died in 1949, the throne passed directly to Princess Charlotte's son, Rainier.

Monaco's fortunes started to revert when Aristotle Onassis turned his attention to the principality. He became a major shareholder of the venerable Société des Bains de Mer, which operated the famous casino as well as Monaco's most important hotels. He also acquired dozens of villas and other buildings, and initiated the renovation of the casino and the harbour as well as the construction of public institutions. He is also rumoured to have had a hand in facilitating the fairytale marriage between Prince Rainier and Grace Kelly which, together with the freshly renovated infrastructure of Monaco, began once again to attract the rich and famous from around the world, and eventually made the principality what it is today – one of the most fascinating and expensive enclaves for the world's elite, who enjoy the local sunshine, zero per-cent crime rate and, last but not least, tax-free status as residents. Today Prince Albert is continuing the successful reign of his father Rainier, and is set on bringing Monaco safely into the twenty-first century.

THE CARIBBEAN SEA: MUSTIQUE

For the past fifty years, the Caribbean Sea has been a favourite playground of the (often) rich and (sometimes) beautiful. Of all the charming islands offering shelter to the sun-deprived during European winters, Mustique is arguably the most refined. From Princess Margaret in the 1960s to Bill Gates, Kate Moss and Tommy Hilfiger today – not forgetting Mick Jagger, who has been a regular for the past forty years – Mustique has for decades been drawing celebrities from all over the world.

Mustique and its inhabitants, however, have not always been so glamorous. Originally discovered in the fifteenth century by Spanish sailors who named them 'Los Pájaros' (or 'the birds' due to their resemblance to a flock of birds in flight), Mustique and its neighbouring islands were later used by pirates to hide their ships and treasure in the sheltered bays. European planters then grew sugar on 'the Grenadines' (as the islands were later re-named), until the development of European sugar crops in the nineteenth century led to the abandonment of Mustique's plantations.

All this changed in the late 1950s when a Scotsman by the name of Colin Christopher Paget Tennant, 3rd Baron Glenconner, arrived on the scene and turned his attention to the jungle and corals that made up Mustique at that time. Before succeeding to the baronetage (other members of this illustrious family have included the aesthete Stephen Tennant and author Emma Tennant), Colin Tennant had been a great traveller and an avid collector. He bought Mustique in 1958 for a pittance, much to the astonishment of his wife who could not quite see the point of owning this piece of wilderness. Tennant, however, had big plans for the island. After building a new village for the inhabitants, planting coconut palms, vegetables and fruit, and developing the island's infrastructure, he began creating building plots for large luxury villas.

In a stroke of genius, he gave one of the finest plots as a wedding gift to HRH Princess Margaret, the sister of Queen Elizabeth II. The newlyweds, Princess Margaret and renowned photographer Lord Snowdon, arrived in 1960 on board the royal yacht *Britannia* to accept their wedding gift. An uncle of Lord Snowdon, the well-known designer Oliver Messel, designed an enchanting villa there, 'Les Jolies Eaux'.

The estate soon became known for its lavish and seemingly never-ending house parties, which delighted the international press (though not necessarily Queen Elizabeth). Tennant's plan worked beautifully, and Princess Margaret's presence soon prompted other notables from around the world to make Mustique 'a home away from home'. The 1960s and '70s saw the meteoric rise of Mustique's fortunes when the beau monde partied and relaxed there *entre eux*, more or less well hidden from the public eye in a very private atmosphere.

Alas, while Tennant, who became Baron Glenconner in the early 1980s, enjoyed the lifestyle he invented, the ongoing cost of running Mustique was quickly depleting his family fortune. He was forced to take on business partners and eventually went 'into exile' on St Lucia.

Mustique, however, continues to thrive. Though no longer a family estate, it has been leased by the Mustique Company, which rents or leases its 89 private villas. One of the secrets of Mustique's success is that it possesses only two privately owned hotels – the small, boutique-style Firefly Hotel, and the larger Cotton House Hotel – thus making it a very private community. One nightspot beloved by locals and high society alike is the legendary Basil's Bar, owned and operated by local entrepreneur Basil Charles, who has been on the island for over thirty years. Mustique's villas continue to be highly sought after, and quickly change hands between the international jetset.

PALM BEACH

In winter, when cities like New York and Chicago are swept by icy winds and blizzards, those of its inhabitants who happen to be blessed with worldly goods tend to migrate in droves to a destination that offers a tropical climate and distinguished surroundings only a short plane-ride away – Palm Beach. Like its more urban sister Miami, Palm Beach was the brainchild of one man – Henry Morrison Flagler.

Flagler mansion, Palm Beach, Florida, c. 1906

Flagler was a picture-book American tycoon, amassing his fortune in oil, railroad development and real estate. Born in 1830 in the small town of Hopewell, New York, he was the son of a poor minister who, after leaving home at fourteen, started his professional career by working in his cousin's store in Bellevue, Ohio, at a salary of $5 per month plus room and board. Flagler's first independent enterprise was anything but a success: the Flagler and York Salt Company collapsed after only three years, causing him to lose his own investment as well as $50,000 he had borrowed from his father-in-law. He was forced to return once again to Bellevue, where he worked in his father-in-law's grain business as a commission merchant. Through this, however, he became acquainted with a man named John D. Rockefeller, who also happened to work as a commission agent and was eager to open an oil refinery – with Flagler as partner. Flagler managed to obtain another loan of $100,000 from his patient father-in-law. Together with chemist and inventor Samuel Andrews, Rockefeller and Flagler founded the enterprise that would become the world-famous Standard Oil. After only five years in operation, the company was the leading oil refinery in America, producing over 10,000 barrels a day. In 1877 Standard Oil moved its headquarters to New York City, and Flagler and his family moved there as well.

Because Flagler's first wife Mary was permanently ill, her doctor advised her to spend the winter in Florida's mild climate. The family travelled in 1878 to Jacksonville, and this seems to have been the start of a lifelong love affair between Florida and Flagler. After Mary died in 1881, Flagler married her former caregiver and they spent their honeymoon in St Augustine, Florida. Flagler soon realized that what the region lacked in hotel facilities, infrastructure and transportation, it made up for in charm and climate. He saw Florida's huge potential to become an attraction for out-of-state visitors.

Although Flagler remained on the Board of Directors of Standard Oil, he gave up his day-to-day involvement in the corporation to pursue his new property interests in Florida. He returned to St Augustine in 1885 and began construction on the 540-room Ponce de Leon hotel. Having been introduced to the quickly developing world of America's railroads by Henry H. Rogers, another key man at

Standard Oil, Flagler shortly thereafter purchased the Jacksonville, St Augustine and Halifax railroad, to support his hotel venture, thus establishing what would become known as 'Flagler's railway' and would be renamed in 1895 the 'Florida East Coast Railway'.

The Hotel Ponce de Leon opened on 10 January 1888 and was an immediate success. Flagler significantly expanded his Florida possessions only two years later. After building a railroad bridge across the St Johns River, and thus gaining access to the southern half of the state, he purchased the Hotel Ormond, just north of Daytona, and built on the shores of Lake Worth the 1,100-room Royal Poinciana Hotel, at the time the largest wooden structure in the world. Two years later, Flagler built the Palm Beach Inn (renamed The Breakers Hotel in 1901), overlooking the Atlantic Ocean in Palm Beach, thus making Palm Beach an instant high-end destination.

Flagler originally intended West Palm Beach to be the terminus of his railroad system. However, in 1894 and 1895, severe freezes hit the area – while only sixty miles to the south, another region was reportedly unharmed. Flagler began considering the idea of developing this area and further extending his railroad system. Local landowners, who spotted a chance to increase the value of their holdings, offered him land in exchange for the establishment of a railroad connection. Flagler's railroad reached Biscayne Bay by 1896. He dredged a channel, built streets, instituted the first water and power systems, and financed the city's first newspaper. When the city was incorporated in 1896, its citizens wanted to honour the man responsible for its growth by naming it Flagler. He declined the honour, persuading them to use instead an old Indian name, 'Miama', and thus the city of Miami was born.

Flagler's second wife Ida Alice had been institutionalized for mental illness since 1895. In 1901, the Florida Legislature passed a bill that made incurable insanity grounds for divorce, opening the way for Flagler to remarry. On August 24 of that year, he married his third wife, Mary Lily Kenan, and the couple soon moved into their new Palm Beach estate, Whitehall, a 55-room Beaux Arts mansion of over 5,500 square metres (60,000 sq. ft), designed by the New York-based firm of Carrère and Hastings, architects of the New York Public Library and the Frick Collection building (see p. 175). With that presence, Flagler set an example for the rest of the East Coast elite to follow. Soon, more and more wealthy Americans were building their winter residences in Palm Beach, thereby establishing once and for all the Palm Beach 'Season' during wintertime.

After falling down a flight of stairs at Whitehall, Flagler died in Palm Beach on 20 May 1913 at the age of 83. The Flagler Monument Island in Biscayne Bay, Flagler College in St Augustine, Flagler County, Florida, and Flagler Beach, Florida, are all testament to the man who 'invented' the state as we know it. Whitehall is nowadays open to the public as the Flagler Museum.

Palm Beach continues to be one of the world's most exclusive communities, where the rich and famous migrate in winter, making it also one of the world's most expensive real-estate markets, with average house prices exceeding the $3 million mark.

TUSCANY

From a geographical standpoint, Tuscany can be described as a hilly region in Central Italy, bordering on the Emilia-Romagna to the north, Liguria to the northwest, the Tyrrhenian Sea to the west, Umbria and Marche to the east, and Lazio to the southeast. From a cultural point of view, however, Tuscany is much more. It is the home of the Italian Renaissance, with its unparalleled heritage of architecture, painting and sculpture, and it is the birthplace of Leonardo da Vinci, Michelangelo and Dante Alighieri alike. Its wines such as Chianti and Brunello di Montalcino, its olive oil, its cuisine, its magical landscape with beautiful towns like Florence, Siena, Pisa, Lucca and San Gimignano are world-renowned. It is little wonder then, that Tuscany is one of the world's most sought-after luxury real-estate markets.

From the eighth century BC – following on from the primitive settlements of the Bronze and Iron Ages – this region was inhabited by the Etruscans. Then, just as in other parts of Europe, the rise of the Roman Empire meant that the territory had to be ceded by the first century BC. Under Roman rule, the cities of Lucca, Pisa, Siena and Florence were founded, and a more sophisticated infrastructure introduced, including a transport network, aqueducts and sewers, and the construction of many buildings, both public and private. After the collapse of the Roman Empire in the fifth century AD, the region – soon to be designated the Duchy of Tuscia – came under the control of the Lombards, the Goths and the Greeks.

Wealth and development were once again brought to the region by the pilgrims travelling along the Via Francigena between Rome and France in medieval times. The food and shelter required by these travellers fuelled the growth of new communities around churches and taverns. When the Holy Roman Empire fell apart in the Middle Ages, the urban centres of northern and central Italy emerged as independent merchant-city republics, the so-called 'communes', birthplaces of the Renaissance. Of particular signifi-

View of Florence with cathedral, Tuscany, c. 1901

cance to Tuscany are the communes of Siena, Pisa, Lucca, Livorno, and of course its foremost driving force, Florence.

In the fifteenth century, Florence extended its rule over neighbouring regions, thus establishing a more or less homogenous zone under the 'Tuscany' banner, by first purchasing Pisa in 1405 (and, not quite as elegantly, brutally suppressing the local resistance there in the following year), and then acquiring Livorno in 1421. Siena proved more 'hard to get', being incorporated into Tuscany only in 1555. Lucca, finally, remained an independent republic until 1847, when it became part of the Grand Duchy of Tuscany as the result of a public referendum.

Florence, Tuscany's leading centre, was from 1434 onwards dominated by the increasingly powerful Medici dynasty. While the roots of the family can be traced back to the twelfth century, the Medicis first appeared in the public eye as influential wool traders in the fourteenth century. A milestone in their meteoric rise was the establishment of the family bank towards the end of the fourteenth century by Giovanni di Bicci de' Medici, the founder of the Florentine family branch. While Giovanni di Bicci created the basis for the legendary wealth of the Medicis (they would later be reputed to be Europe's - and thus the world's – richest family), he was not particularly interested in politics unless his own bank was directly concerned. This changed under his son, Cosimo. Cosimo used the huge financial power of his bank to influence the politics of Florence on many levels without, however, holding any official office. This, of course, did not go unnoticed by the old, established Florentine families such as the Albizzis, who managed to have him first imprisoned and then exiled. Cosimo, however, took his bank with him into exile, thus draining Florence of considerable financial resources. When more and more capital followed him, Florence was forced to lift the exile. Upon his return, Cosimo worked steadily to consolidate his position. Although the Florentine republic continued to exist on paper, Cosimo in effect 'ruled' it through his financial power and widespread loyal network. More than just a financial genius and gifted power politician, Cosimo was also a wise, patriotic ruler whose primary aim was to strengthen and grow Florence's political but also cultural power. He was an unequalled patron of the arts, who drew many artists to Florence and made it the birthplace of the Renaissance movement. This made him a true 'godfather' of Florence, a status that was officially recognized upon his death when the title 'Pater Patriae', 'Father of the Country', was carved on his tombstone in the Church of San Lorenzo.

Cosimo's legacy was continued under his son Piero (the Gouty) and especially his gifted grandson Lorenzo (the Magnificent). Under these patrons, Florence and Tuscany became the epicentre of the Florentine Renaissance. There were plenty of setbacks during the early rule of the Medici dynasty: political plots, assassination attempts (Lorenzo's brother Giuliano was in fact murdered) and ongoing disputes with the Pope were, more or less, common occurrences. However, the ascent of the family was unstoppable. One of Lorenzo's sons, Giuliano II, became the first noble member of the family as the Duke of Nemours; his brother Giovanni became Pope Leo X, the first of three Popes the Medici family would eventually produce. Under Pope Clement VII and Emperor Charles V, Alessandro de' Medici finally emerged as the first formally appointed hereditary ruler of the Medici family, the first 'Duke of Tuscany'. He was succeeded by Cosimo I, who established for himself and his successors the title of 'Grand Duke of Tuscany'. For the next two hundred years, generations of the Medici family would rule Tuscany as Grand Dukes.

The Medicis presided over some of the most important times of Tuscany's economic and cultural growth. Under their patronage, sciences and arts flowered, spreading the ideas of the Renaissance movement all over the world for centuries to come (the Medicis were patrons of, among others, Botticelli, Michelangelo and Leonardo da Vinci). On the economic side, Tuscany underwent some fundamental changes. Many of its traditional industries, such as the wool industry, declined and were replaced by trade and 're-feudalization' which saw many patricians investing in land instead of industry. By the early eighteenth century, however, Tuscany was in steady decline under the rule of the last Medici grand dukes.

During the following centuries the Grand Duchy of Tuscany saw a series of changes in ownership. After the main branch of the Medici family died out with Gian Castone, Tuscany became a possession of the house of Habsburg-Lorraine, rulers of neighbouring Austria. Leopold I – son of the first new ruler of Tuscany, Francis of Lorraine – reformed it quite drastically during his long reign, abolishing the last remaining traces of serfdom and making it once more one of the most prosperous Italian states. His successor, Ferdinand III, however, had the misfortune to be dispossessed in 1801 by Napoleon Bonaparte, who required that Tuscany be given to the Bourbon Dukes of Parma to compensate them for the loss of their own duchy. To make that compensation more palatable, the Grand Duchy of Tuscany was re-styled the kingdom of Etruria. In 1807, however, Napoleon once again had other plans for Tuscany/Etruria and annexed it to his French empire (in 1809 he gave his sister Elisa the honorary title of Grand Duchess of Tuscany). In 1814, after Napoleon's downfall, Ferdinand III was restored as grand duke. However, in 1815, the Congress of Vienna separated the Duchy of Lucca from Tuscany to give it, again, to the Bourbons of Parma in compensation for other losses. In 1848, Tuscany became, once again, a republic for a brief period of time as a result of the political upheavals and ensuing revolutions all over Europe. However, former ruler Leopold II was quickly restored as Grand Duke in 1849 to rule again for another ten years before handing over to his successor Ferdinand IV. Ferdinand's reign, however, was equally short-lived, as in 1860 Tuscany became part of Italy.

During Tuscany's long and colourful history, it has always attracted visitors from across the globe, many of whom also settled there. Its most important heritage with regard to residential architecture undoubtedly dates back to the Renaissance period; its Renaissance villas influenced architects all over the world. The original properties from this period continue to be highly sought-after, only rarely available on the open market, often quickly and sometimes secretly changing hands for considerable sums of money. The most in-demand examples tend to be found between the traditional centres of Tuscany – Florence, Siena, Pisa, Lucca and Livorno.

In recent times, the much more rustic, smaller sisters of those villas – the so-called 'rustici' ('rustico' means 'farmhouse') – have become frequent alternative choices. Traditional farmhouses are increasingly being converted into large country houses, adapted to the tastes of today's buyers. Multiple bedrooms and bathrooms, luxurious kitchens and generous pools now grace properties in which only fifty years ago sheep, cows and corn were stored. Prices for these converted farmhouses often break the €1 million barrier, making them a staple of the current Tuscan luxury real-estate market.

GSTAAD AND ST MORITZ

The winter sporting activities of the rich and famous are often associated with two places in Switzerland – Gstaad and St Moritz.

Gstaad is located in the Bernese 'Oberland' in the Swiss Alps. For centuries, it was a tiny mountain village probably best known for its independent, not to say stubborn, inhabitants. All this changed when winter sports became fashionable in the early twentieth century. To cater to the new clientele, luxurious hotels sprang up all over the countryside, and Gstaad was no exception. 1913 saw the grand opening of the 'Royal Hotel, Winter & Gstaad Palace', offering 150 rooms with luxuries such as fifty private bathrooms, electrical lighting throughout and six telephone booths. The hotel boomed and attracted a distinguished international clientele that firmly put Gstaad on the map as a high-society winter destination. Before long, entertainers such as Maurice Chevalier, Louis Armstrong and Ella Fitzgerald were performing at the Gstaad Palace.

In the 1950s, some of the Gstaad regulars felt the need to create an environment where they could be among themselves and keep their distance from the common tourist. Thus, in 1957, the Eagle Ski Club was born. Eighty-one founding members created a private haven on the heights of Gstaad, the first president of the club being the Earl of Warwick, followed some years later by Vicomte Charles Benoît d'Azy. Subsequent presidents have included Count Edouard Decazes and Prince Nicolas Romanoff.

An added attraction of Gstaad is the fact that it houses one of the most exceptional school campuses in the world – the winter site of the legendary boarding school Le Rosey. Established in 1880, the 'Institut Le Rosey' (not to be confused with its rival, the 'Institut auf dem Rosenberg' in St Gallen) is the oldest private boarding school in Switzerland and one of the most exclusive private schools in the world. While Le Rosey's summer campus, the Château du Rosey, in the village of Rolle between Geneva and Lausanne, is undoubtedly pleasant, the real clincher is the winter campus – the Chalet Rex in Gstaad. Annual fees and other charges easily add up to CHF 100,000 per year, thus ensuring a rather exclusive mix of pupils. Le Rosey's

View of St Moritz, c. 1890

alumni list reads like a mixture of the *Almanac de Gotha* and a high-society magazine: former pupils include the Aga Khan, the Crown Prince of Yugoslavia, two Belgian kings, the last king of Egypt, Prince Rainier III of Monaco and the Grand Duke of Luxembourg, as well as members of the Stavros Niarchos, Rothschild, Taittinger and Ferragamo families. All these pupils ensure that the world's elite make an early, and often unforgettable, acquaintance with Gstaad, prompting many of them to return in later years.

Needless to say, many of these pupils and/or seasonal visitors have wanted to own a place in this mountain heaven. Gstaad is often regarded as one of the most luxurious, yet at the same time most discreet winter-sport havens. With a population of only 2,500 inhabitants, a pedestrian zone in the heart of the village, and homogenous building structures, Gstaad exudes 'understated luxury'. Rainier III of Monaco and his wife Grace Kelly were among the many illustrious chalet owners there. Very few of the highly sought-after chalets ever come on the open market, as they tend to (quickly and discreetly) change hands between the members of international high society. Notable residents have included Roger Moore, Ursula Andress, Tina Turner, Ernesto Bertarelli, Bernie Ecclestone, Elle Macpherson and members of various European royal families.

Gstaad's arch rival is undoubtedly St Moritz in the Swiss canton of Graubünden. St Moritz (with the accent on the 'i' in 'Moritz') actually consists of four different quarters, namely St Moritz-Dorf, St Moritz-Bad, Suvretta and part of Champfer; however, as every habitué of St Moritz will be happy to tell you, only St Moritz-Dorf on the northern shore of Lake St Moritz is regarded as 'the real thing'. Skiing is done mostly on the Corviglia mountain.

St Moritz's modern history began with the opening of its first hotel, the Kulm Hotel. At that time St Moritz was regarded as a summer destination, but this changed when hotelier Johannes Badrutt entered into a wager with four visiting Englishmen. He offered to put them up in his hotel for free during the winter season and let them stay as long as they liked: should they not enjoy St Moritz in the winter, he would pay them back all their travel expenses. The English accepted and … stayed from Christmas until Easter. Soon St Moritz became a fashionable winter resort for European high society, enabling Badrutt to open a 'Grand Hotel', the now renowned Badrutt Palace.

The town soon established some rather extraordinary traditions. During the winter season of 1884–85, the famous St Moritz Tobogganing Club was founded by a number of well-heeled British expats. Since then, the legendary Cresta Run has offered its privileged members the dubious honour of sliding down an icy bob-run on a flimsy skeleton-sled, risking life and limb in the process. A further unusual attraction is the 'White Turf', a series of horse races conducted every winter on the frozen St Moritz lake. And, of course, where an ordinary horse race can be conducted, one may as well play polo. Since 1985 'Polo on Snow' has been a staple of the winter circuit, also attracting international high society to St Moritz.

With over 5,000 inhabitants, St Moritz is often seen as the livelier sister to the more discreet Gstaad. Whereas in Gstaad a chalet is de rigueur, St Moritz offers a broader choice of high-end accommodation. An apartment in the Palace Hotel, for example, is one of the most prestigious places to lay one's head. In addition to traditional houses and chalets, St Moritz also offers more unusual options. For example, British star architect Lord Norman Foster has created Chesa Futura, a round structure on stilts, totally covered in locally sourced wood. Its six apartments, with up to ten rooms, have been an immediate success with international buyers and have become a desirable alternative to more traditional choices.

AFTERWORD

'If these walls had ears…' is a saying I like a lot – I guess because it applies so well to my home of the past thirty years, Bled Targui in Marrakech, Morocco. Homes always reflect the personality and the history of their owners, and that's exactly why we all love to have a look 'behind the scenes' of a home – to find out more about the people who live there; what their story, what their history is.…

My home, Bled Targui, has a particularly colourful history to tell. Once an oasis of the famous Tuareg tribe, it has been my second home for many years, the estate having originally been given to my father-in-law, Alfried Krupp von Bohlen und Halbach, by His Majesty King Hassan II of Morocco. In the 1970s my husband, Arndt Krupp von Bohlen und Halbach, had Bled Targui built as a residence.

Bled Targui is still an oasis, where I – and thousands of beautiful birds – have our refuge. Of course 'beings' of another kind have also laid their head in my *gemütlich* home. From Rolling Stones to royalty, I have had the privilege of entertaining a wide array of friends and guests.

I am thrilled to have Bled Targui included in this fascinating book. I hope that you, just like me, have not been able to stop turning the pages, marvelling at these captivating homes and reading the incredible stories!

Love,

Henriette von Bohlen und Halbach,
née Princess von Auersperg

ACKNOWLEDGMENTS

The author wishes to thank the following individuals and organizations for their generous support in producing this volume and their kind permission to use the stunning photography in this book:

Foreword: Donald J. Trump. **1. The Downtown Loft:** Ed Bazinet and Wouter Deruytter; Stephen L. McRae, Sotheby's International Realty New York. **2. Relaxed Island Living:** George Damianos, Damianos Sotheby's International Realty. **3. 1001 Nights Dream:** Tine Hagemaster, Kristina Szekely Sotheby's International Realty. **4. Grand Hotel Heaven:** Meredyth Hull Smith, Sotheby's International Realty New York. **5. Provençal Paradise:** Dr. Peter G. Gollmer. **6. Traditional Island Living:** George Damianos, Damianos Sotheby's International Realty. **7. A Grand London Residence (and p. 23):** Charles Smith, Sotheby's International Realty London. **8. The Moroccan Oasis (and p. 190):** I.D. Henriette von Bohlen und Halbach. **9. The French Château Revisited:** Dominique Mandonnaud; Jean-Baptiste Isambert. **10. The Neo-Palladian Villa:** Tine Hagemaster, Kristina Szekely Sotheby's International Realty. **11. The English Country House:** Dieter Klostermann. **12. A Palace in an Apartment:** Mr and Mrs Marty Richards; Nikki Fields, Sotheby's International Realty New York. **13. The Spanish Colonial Mansion (and p. 8):** Cristina B. Condon, Sotheby's International Realty Palm Beach. **14. The Perfect Pied-à-Terre:** Charles Smith, Sotheby's International Realty London. **15. A Seaside Penthouse:** Anne Maria Jagdfeld. **16. The Frank Lloyd Wright Icon:** Virginia Lovness; Kimberly Falker and Mollie Windmiller, SKY Sotheby's International Realty. **17. A Fairytale Castle:** Paul de Vilder; Herbert Ypma. **18. The Neutra Masterpiece:** Vidal Sassoon; Barry Sloane, Sotheby's International Realty Beverly Hills. **19. The Country Retreat:** Annemarie DiPasquale, Daniel Gale Sotheby's International Realty. **20. The Big One:** Donald J. Trump; Cristina B. Condon, Sotheby's International Realty Palm Beach. **Afterword:** I.D. Henriette von Bohlen und Halbach.

Picture credits: p. 7 The Trump Organization; p. 10 Marbella Club Hotel, Golf Resort & Spa, Spain; p. 11 Sotheby's International Realty France; p. 12 (above) English Heritage; p. 12 (below) Photo © Fototeca Unione; p. 13 from *Strongholds of the Realm* by Charles Knightly, Thames & Hudson Ltd, London, 1979; p. 14 (above) Photo © Hugh Palmer from *The Formal Garden: Traditions of Art and Nature* by Mark Laird, Thames & Hudson Ltd, London, 1992; p. 14 (below) Photo Carrieri; p. 19 40 Bond Street Partners LLC, c/o Ian Schrager Company; p. 20 Sciame Development, Inc.; p. 169 (right) Landmarks Preservation Council of Illinois; p. 170 Library of Congress, Prints & Photographs Division, HABS PA, 46 – ARD, 2-3; p. 175 Library of Congress, Prints and Photographs Division, Detroit Publishing Company Collection; p. 179 Library of Congress, Prints and Photographs Division; p. 180 Library of Congress, Prints and Photographs Division, Detroit Publishing Company Collection; p. 182 Kraft family archive; p. 183 Library of Congress, Prints and Photographs Division, Detroit Publishing Company Collection; p. 186 Library of Congress, Prints and Photographs Division, Detroit Publishing Company Collection; p. 187 Library of Congress, Prints and Photographs Division; p. 189 Library of Congress, Prints and Photographs Division, Detroit Publishing Company Collection; p. 191 I.D. Henriette von Bohlen und Halbach.

Every effort has been made to locate and credit copyright holders of the material reproduced in this book. The author and publisher apologize for any omissions or errors, which can be corrected in future editions.

Thank you

Prof. Dr. Volker and Regine Kraft for your loving faith, trust and support: without you Cambridge, La Jolla and Fortitude AG would not have been possible. Sibylle 'Cat' Mueller for hunting with me in the jungle. Bertie for completing our family. 964 aka Zackary W. Wright for his friendship across the oceans. 'Uncle' Peter Blond for being the Field Marshall's chief transport advisor.

The entire team at Thames & Hudson, London, especially Jamie Camplin, and my editor Jenny Wilson and designer Karin Fremer. Toodle-oh, pip pip!